A
WARRIOR
MARRIED TO HIS WIFE
AND PTSD

CURTIS BUTLER III

ISBN 978-1-0980-2331-7 (paperback)
ISBN 978-1-0980-2332-4 (digital)

Christian Faith Publishing, Inc.
832 Park Avenue
Meadville, PA 16335
www.christianfaithpublishing.com

While the author has made every effort to provide accurate accounts of all events and internet addresses at the time of this publication, either the publisher or the author assumes any responsibility for errors or for changes that may occur after publication.

Printed in the United States of America

A Warrior Married to his Wife and PTSD
Book Consultants
(Retired ARMY)
LTC Kevin Gainer
Dr. Emily Butler Anderson and Attorney Charles Singleton

Thank You to my Pastors Dr. Terrance and Elaine Gattis of
Mount Olive Baptist Church for meeting with my wife and
I about "A Warrior Married to His Wife and PTSD".

A Warrior Married to his Wife and PTSD

We all say good morning to others.
But do you really mean it?
Do you know the meaning of "good morning"? Let me help you.
Get up.
Open your heart for love.
Open your mind for understanding.
Dedicate your day to God.
Meditate on God's Word.
Optimise your faith and hope.
Rebuke all evils.
Never doubt God's love.
Inspire someone to be the best human.
Nothing should scare you, your Father is a king.
Go out with joy and peace.
Good morning and have a blessed day! Hooah!

No weapon formed against me shall prosper, for my righteousness is of the Lord. And whatever I do will prosper for I'm like a tree that's planted by the rivers of water.

—Isaiah 54:17, Psalms 1:3

To my military family:

Thank you for your dedication, time, and selflessness service to your family, friends and all mankind. I appreciate what you do around the world. I pray for each and every one of you for your safe return and that you receive many blessings. To my fallen comrades, I miss, think, and pray for you and your families daily. Yes, I cry like a baby since that hurt is so very deep in my bones soul and spirit. May you continue to rest in Gods' arms, *hooah*!

CONTENTS

Preface...13
Introduction...15
A Warrior Marries His Warrior..21

Chapter 1:   My Rib...23
Chapter 2:   Who Can You Trust at the VA or Regional Office...28
Chapter 3:   The Vet Center...37
Chapter 4:   The Different Men I Brought to the Bedroom........46
Chapter 5:   PTSD Does Not Mean You are Stupid...................49
Chapter 6:   Veterans and Family Members of
              Veterans Speak Out.......................................60
Chapter 7:   God, Can we Talk?..94
Chapter 8:   *Denied* is Not a Bad Word...............................98
Chapter 9:   Inspirational Quotes and Sayings.......................118
Chapter 10:   Migraine..120
Chapter 11:   Coping Skills that Get me through the Day..........132
Chapter 12:   The Director's Office...................................134
Chapter 13:   Are VA Employees Robbing Taxpayers
              and Disabled Veterans?..................................136

Acknowledgments...203
Resources for Attorneys...211
Emergency Telephone Numbers...215

PREFACE

This book you are about to read was written by a veteran and his wife who are still fighting a war while back on the home turf after fighting for *freedom* of the *American* people for which this soldier raised his right hand once in 1989 before going to Fort Jackson, South Carolina, and again in 2001 at Fort Gillem, Georgia. This veteran, like many others before him, struggle with doctor appointments at the VA Hospital in Decatur, Georgia, and all over with the complexity of the suicide hotline, from tape-recording doctors and then reading the notes, which were totally different; filing paperwork at the regional office in Decatur, Georgia, with the different federal employees assigned to the disabled American veterans (DAV), who gave me the run around with misinformation; or losing of vital paperwork, which delays or drops your claims, making you go through that tedious process all over again while they still collect a paycheck. This also includes the raters who scheme over vital information that they ask you for, to deny or say it was not worded properly as I spoke to them over the phone, not the raters but people in the director's office level. My question is why is it that your PTSD have to be written down a certain way in order for it to be correct? The military as in all statements *who*, *what*, *when*, *where*, *why*, and *how*. Is this too good for the same government that sent us to *war*?

Flashbacks, intrusive emotions, night terrors, explosive outburst, irritabilities, with suicidal and homicidal tendencies that frightens my wife and daughter that live with a man who is supposed to protect them. I cry and cry and do not know why I am crying. My wife holds me as if she is nursing a baby and tells me it's going to be all right; help is on the way. Our government to our health care provider and veteran representatives, you beat us down so bad and we see the "I do not care" on your faces. Again, you continue to run us in like herds of cattle until the media pops up, you do a quick fix then when the media leaves, you go back to business as usual.

Congress, we need to communicate better with the veterans and family members about Title 38 Federal Rules and Regulation and (COVA) Courts of Veterans Appeals so that these veterans and family members can have a better chance on the battlefield here in the states on receiving their benefits.

Fighting for your *freedoms* so that you could continue receiving your benefits for *life*, while we beg for crumbs is disgraceful, UN American and sickening. I pray every night that our super rich government treat these war *heroes* who do not get paid six figures for the rest of their lives to afford us to live comfortably with our families and to eliminate the red tape of injustice.

Why is it when a veteran with 50 percent or higher for their disabilities go to an outside hospital, being they do not live close to the VA Hospital, receives a bill and then send to the fee basis office, and it takes forever for our government to make payments? Many veterans are receiving bad credit due to this setup. Why does the government not have funds set aside for these types of issues? It would help us out in a major way that makes it seem to our creditors that we are not responsible. Again we are just asking for a hand up.

INTRODUCTION

Life in Baghdad, Iraq, in October 2003 and again in 2006 was like living in a Crock-Pot; it was hot, and the breeze, if you can call it, that was just as hot. We would travel to strange destinations to attend meetings, drop off supplies, or pick up soldiers. We even performed guard duty, and with the scrooching temperatures, our protective gear we wore added about twenty degrees and an extra thirty pounds. The temperature was approximately one hundred forty degrees or better; I was told to put on some suntan lotion, and I thought the officer was making a joke because I did not know a black man could get a sun burn in the desert. This is to be true.

When on missions as the driver or gunner or (PSD) protective security detail assigned to General Dempsey, we came across good, bad, and scared Iraqis in their own country. The good and scared Iraqis want change and peace between the others who are still trying to live in the past. They want schools so that they can be educated and receive a good job in order to maintain the things needed to take care of their families. When stationed out in Iraq, change was being made slowly but surely, as you know change takes a while.

Every time before leaving off the base in Iraq, I would pray that we get to and from our location safe; many times, we hear shots fired and would try to get what location it was coming from so that we could assist. If a call came through over the radio, we were lucky or prayed up. Other soldiers were not so lucky making the worldwide news as being a casualty or received injuries. Even if we did not know that soldier, it did not matter, we were family whether you like the person or not. I would tell whoever I was doing security for, "My job is to bring you back dead or alive, but you will be back."

15

When soldiers sacrifice their lives for another person in a distant land or even people they do not know, they are considered my *heroes* and will never be forgotten. So when waking up every morning, thank God for these very special people like angels protecting our way of life, and please pray for the families and units of these fine warriors, they deserve the best of the best because of what they do.

We can help our soldiers also by sending care packages from schools, churches, organizations, etc. Soldiers like pictures from children because we feel a need to protect them. The smiles on their faces are priceless. These things make it feel like home a little bit. If possible, send calling cards so that we can call loved ones from time to time.

Guard duty was my primary job on my second tour in Tal Afar, Iraq. Some nights were scary because the entire city would go dark, and you could not see your hands in front of you. You had to have light discipline; this was so snipers could not pick you off or know your location. We had Iraqi officers wanting to come on the base with loaded weapons, ambulance approximately a thousand feet from us wanting to enter and use our hospital. Incidents like these could have been deadly situations. We drew down weapons in this situation until higher-ups came to assist with the Iraqi officers unloading their weapons. The driver in the ambulance, he took off, but we had eyes on him and to take him down if he try to drive through our barricade with the M-249s (SAW) squad automatic weapon that shoots approximately 600 rounds per minute; and the M-249B (SAW) squad automatic weapon, that shoots approximately 750 rounds per minute; along with some M4s, which shoots approximately 750 to 900 rounds per minute; and the M203 grenade launcher, which is capable of firing high-explosive dual purpose rounds, high-explosive rounds, Nato high-explosive, smoke, and illumination grenades.

Guard duty could go from eight hours on, depending if they were short on personnel or if a mission was going on. I felt good about my job because we were the first means of defense, and we took this seriously because of security at other locations that where breached, ending in the kidnapping, torture, and killings of soldiers.

I have been to more memorial services while in Iraq in one year than anyone on the civilian side that I know.

I always wonder why we have rules in a war zone; the enemies love this. I was told by higher-ups that if they point their weapons at us, we are not supposed to shoot unless they shoot at us first (if that's not post-traumatic stress, what is?). If you are dead, you cannot shoot back. Then our government arrest soldiers for an over kill of the enemy. Well, when an improvised explosive device takes out a couple of soldiers, don't you think that's an overkill when the casket comes home empty? Ladies and gentlemen of congress, would you like to go on a ride along with these fine men and women of our military and get the feel of rounds whizzing past you? Or a rocket attack? Or mortar rounds hitting around you? If you did, then you would see a lot different through the eyes of a soldier or a *marine*.

Our soldiers have every right to protect themselves and families; they should not be ridiculed if they have a disability, remember our country sent us in harm's way in order for our country to be free. When Soldiers go into harm's way, our government need to ensure the family members are provided with mental health professions for the entire fifteen months or as many times the family member goes into harm's way. Soldiers should have mental health professions waiting for them in Kuwait, speaking to the soldiers of the traumatic occurrences they went through. Come on, America, let us help these *heroes* out and not think about me, me, me all the time.

America, our soldiers are doing a magnificent job, and we, as a country, need to stand with these *heroes* as they return to the country they love and fight for. If not, we are no better than the Iraqis that have fallen by the waste side many years ago. Let us not keep up this revolving door that never shuts. We need to ensure our *heroes* receive their disabilities when leaving the service. I always hear this is a voluntary service, but don't you voluntarily enjoy going from point *A* to point *B*. Wake up, America; we're falling behind. If these soldiers did not fight and go into harm's way whether right or wrong, we would probably be slave in our own country like the Iraqi people are; they want to be free like us.

We were being attacked one of many nights at approximately 20:00 hours or 8:00 p.m. on (FOB) forward operation base (BIAP) Baghdad International Airport. I had a severe migraine going to the concrete bunker. As the all clear was called, I was told as I'm walking back to my tent with other soldiers, and someone said man down. I must have blacked out and hit my head because after that, it got real quiet, like I was the only one there at the time. When I came through, I was on a Black Hawk in route to the *cash unit*, which is our military hospital. As I'm lying on the gurney facing up, I see rounds coming close to the Black Hawk as the pilots fly totally in the dark, and I remember speaking with God, saying if it's time for me to go I don't want to feel anything. I thought about *Black Hawk Down*, tears roll down my face as I am strapped in, not able to move knowing that I may be seeing my heavenly father real soon. We were getting heavy fire from the Iraqi insurgents.

Some soldiers from another outfit came to swap vehicles and get parts from our maintenance people. The following week, some of those soldiers got killed in a (IED) improvised explosive device attack, transferring supplies to another (FOB). It was like we knew these soldiers for years but really, it was a couple of days. I didn't have time to mourn, but I prayed for them and their families because my team had a mission; we were headed out, and I had to have a clear mind as my team headed outside the (FOB) into a jungle full of insurgents, waiting to capture or kill a soldier as a prize. If a soldier was captured or killed by an Iraqi, they received money from insurgents and sometimes display the soldier or anyone working with US coalition in a gruesome and inhumane way.

I was at the front gate when I noticed an army captain chasing a black Mercedes Benz without his weapon drawn, running full sprint. I ran right up on him as the car stopped. When we stopped, he saw that my M4 was trained on the vehicle and an Abram's Tank rolled up and placed their barrel on the window of the car. The captain told me thanks. I said, "Sir, I saw that your weapon wasn't drawn, so I wanted to make sure you were covered."

He replied, "Roger that!" Just that fast, he forgot where he was at. Four insurgents where detained.

When my tour was over, I went back home to visit family and friends as well to meet my dad at the 369th infantry regiment "Harlem Hellfighters" national guard armory in Harlem, New York. They were loading up and getting ready to head out to Fort Dix, New Jersey, for their tour of duty in Baghdad, Iraq. Once we got there and his unit was lock down until they head out, I briefed my dad along with some of his soldiers on the dangers. For instance, I told them, "If you didn't put it down, don't pick it up. The insurgents love to place booby traps. You will also be on the road to BIAP which is IED alley, make sure you place sandbags on the floor of all of your vehicles, scan your area, and be at the ready. When getting out of your vehicles, watch your step. If there is a full moon, it will brighten up the sky which lets the insurgents see movement on the base clearly. You will have incoming of rockets, mortar rounds, and small arms fire. At approximately 20:00 hours or 8:00 p.m. On some days, you will get attacked with rockets, mortar rounds, and small arms fire. On Holidays, mornings and afternoon, you will get attacked. Keep your vehicles well maintained and your weapons cleaned and eat right and drinking plenty of water and pray."

I said be safe, and I told my dad, "Love you, Man."

And he said, "Love you too."

My dad's unit got to Kuwait and got causalities. And when they arrived in Baghdad, Iraq, they had causalities on the IED alley which I briefed them on. I walked past some of those soldiers at the *armory*, and I still have the news article of those incidents, and I sit back with tears in my eyes and thank them for their service to our country.

Rest in peace to all of the soldiers and *marines* who gave all for freedom and peace! Your tour has ended, *rest*!

A WARRIOR MARRIES
HIS WARRIOR

Marrying a veteran with PTSD is not for everyone. Should you marry someone with PTSD? Only God can answer that question. Never enter into battle without him leading you. He has to lead and equip you, or you will lose. God has been preparing me for this battle since I was nine years old when he called me into prayer to intercede for my family.

When I was nine years old, God would wake me up in the middle of the night and say, "Pray for protection." When I began to pray, I would feel an evil force enter the front door of the house. You may ask why the prayers didn't stop the evil force from entering the house. Weapons formed but that don't prosper (prevail). 26 years later, when I overheard my mom talking to my nephew, it was confirmed that the weapon did not prevail. What she described that entered my mom and dad's bedroom was what I felt when I was called to intercede. The evil force did no harm. I have been called into prayer to intercede for others as well. I am no stranger to battle. But I only battle when the Holy Spirit beckons me. I don't volunteer.

In 2013, when I married, Curtis Butler III, a veteran with PTSD, I knew that I was going into battle. I did not voluntarily enlist. I was called. There have been times when I questioned God and Curtis why was I chosen to be Curtis' wife and warrior? He said, "You are anointed for this."

I said, "I could have prayed from a distance." Conclusion: God wanted a warrior with Curtis on a daily basis that he can count on when he calls. He wanted a warrior for a warrior, a veteran.

What has life been like married to a veteran with PTSD? There have been mountain top and valley experiences. God has and will always be with me through it all.

During the valley experiences, Curtis is irritable, moody, overly critical, and extremely angry, stays up all night, experiences flashbacks, and is depressed. I find it is best not to go in the "war zone" with him. He is loaded with ammunition. I have to be loaded with prayer on the home front. Psalm 23:4 says, "Yea, though I walk through the valley of the shadow of death, I will fear no evil: for thou art with me; thy rod and thy staff they comfort me." To have a shadow, you have to have light. Jesus is the light (John 8:12). There is no way out of the valley except going through. It may be a long walk or a short walk. The length of the walk depends on how many memories surfaces during the PTSD episode. Don't forget your armor while you are walking through the valley. You will find the armor you need in Ephesians 6:10–18.

CHAPTER 1

My Rib

Caregiver, Wife, and Babysitter

I met my rib at church in 2012. She was the cutest little lady I saw. I really didn't want to say anything because I was ashamed and frightened of the disorder I brought back home with me. I've had relationships that I didn't pursue as a result of I was scared and didn't want to bring anyone into my crazy life and have those thinking ill will toward me. But Tatina had this heart that said I'm built for this assignment, and we started dating. I was trying to get my life back and prayed that I do not mess her life up and her daughter. Lord knows I had plenty on my plate. I figured, me speaking about being homeless twice in the same year, that Tatina would say I manage my fund poorly, but instead she told me she was homeless also, and she's looking at this businesswoman and saying go figure how is a veteran of this great country homeless. Tatina didn't run from me; we prayed for one another and we enjoyed each other's company. While dating, she noticed certain signs that I didn't notice, but she stuck with me. As we look toward the wedding day, we still had some hard time with my mood swings, not caring, being a failure as a *man,* thinking I'm sucking up air someone worthy should be having, why me.

May 25, 2013, Memorial Day weekend, Tatina and I got married in front of approximately 147 family and friends and wow what a day. I couldn't believe that this was actually happening. I finally got my rib and through thick and thin, she will be by my side as one. Some days, were harder than others, dealing with me not sleeping for three or four nights, crying and don't even know why I'm crying. Sometimes when Tatina is speaking with me and then ask me question about what we've spoken about, I would be lost and confused trying to remember what she said, and I would get frustrated being I couldn't remember, and I would get furious. Tatina deals with the many side effects of the medicine I take. It's been over a hundred different prescribed pills. I tell her I feel like a junkie waiting to die, and Tatina will say I didn't marry you so you could die on me. I know Curtis Butler III will never return again for my resume of life has changed, and I also see it changing my wife. Now she has the stressors of Post-Traumatic Stress Disorder. Sometimes, I think I bit of too much to chew, since I'm trying to figure me out and figure my new life with a wife and teenage daughter in the house. I'm learning every day, and at the same time, I want to die for the sake of I feel that no one wants to help or just don't care. People that are reading this may say I have my wife and daughter, sometimes I get it and sometimes I don't.

My rib told me after she had her surgery that I came out the front door in a rage when a policeman drove up in the driveway, and that she pulled me back considering I had an episode. The cop told my wife to come outside, and she told me she said I need a supervisor and that the cop was drawing his weapon. Tatina told me that cop will not kill my husband, and that I was having a flashback due to the pipes bursting in the kitchen, which made it look like a JDAM or improvised explosive device hit. There are many incidents where the police cordon the block until I regained focus before they let the emergency medical team come inside the house.

I despise what's happening around me; it's like a never ending merry-go-round that just doesn't stop. I am going to therapy and all doctor appointments at the VA, even though I don't trust them, and my wife don't like going there on the grounds that she feels the doctors try to overtake the conversation instead of listening and just feed you medicine instead of getting to the root of the problem. I do go to an outside doctor that is close to me since I live fifty miles away from the VA, but I go when I have appointments. Thank God for Medicare in view of my wife likes when I can go the hospital or an urgent care.

The majority of our date night is the hospital and urgent care, but when things are a little normal around the Butler house, we may go get a bite to eat, and I always sit looking at the front door and watching other people eat. I will not go to a movie theater. I get a panic attack, racing heartbeat, and teary-eyed, and my wife loves to go to the movies, so she goes alone or with her girlfriends. I would give anything to take my wife to the movies and wrap my arm around her and enjoy each other's company.

At times, my wife wants to throw in the towel, whereas the stress of being a caregiver, wife, and babysitter, it's a job in a half with no time off and plenty of overtime. I have to remind myself that we are on the same team, at times, I think she's not but that's when I'm not in my right mind. If it wasn't for my wife, you wouldn't be reading none of this right now. In view of she informs me of everything that happens, even recording my rants that I have. Lord, I do not like this new upgrade that is a part of my life. I'm not speaking of my wife and my kids. I'm speaking of the sleepless nights, cold sweats, anger, over medicated, not known who I am, stress, depressed, suicidal with homicidal tendencies, seeing soldier when I sleep or awake that have given their all for this country.

At times, I would like to erase my resume that is a part of me so that I could be happy again, but we do not have a magic wand or a potion, but I work on myself as much as possible with the help of my wife, family, and close friends, which are mostly veterans due to we understand one another, and we don't point the finger or look at each other side ways as if we are a bad germ. My wife will pick up on things to make sure I didn't go off into space being at times my mind wanders when I don't want to. I call this my blackout moment or stage reason being once I'm all the way in; I see nothing and everything gets dark. What seems like hours appears to be minutes and then I return back from what I still don't know.

I'm mostly a homebody and like being by myself, seemly strange but married to my wife and PTSD, this is true. I even ride out by myself trying to enjoy what I came back home to. Sometimes, my wife and I will ride out some place, and I would have to force myself to let my guard down, but God is still working on me with that one. My wife likes to hold hands, but I want my hands free just in case something kicks off. I could better protect her if need be. One thing I love about my wife, man, she is a fighter. She was the one pushing me to get my medical records in order and pushing me to write this book with the help my editor friends and my wife. My wife said the world needs to hear that we need help. Stop right there; my wife didn't say I need help she said we. I'm glad that plenty of people are behind me, but my *rib* is right by my side through the good and bad times.

Tatina and I started a new hobby together which is saving in gold by the grams, which will bless the future of our children's children. This is to keep me semi busy, or you may say distracted. This way, we get to spend some time together and really get to continue finding out who we are. Most of the times if I'm not schedule for a VA appointment, I'm just in the bedroom, staring off in space asking, "Did you see that running across the room?"

Her response is no then I find myself searching for it. My wife would say it was my imagination, okay imagination, but I know I saw something. After that episode, Tatina would try to change my mindset; sometimes it works sometimes it doesn't. I give my rib an *A* plus because she helps me try to relax, smile, and to see life through her beautiful brown eyes. So we'd go for a drive or walk, and her favorite, get a bite to eat. Now, this is where the hobby kicks in most of the time. We would ask our waiter or waitress if they have gold in their financial portfolio and a hundred percent of the time they say no. I thought gold was brought in ounces. Then either Tatina or I would say they can get it in one, two point five, and five grams of twenty-four-karat gold, 999.9% delivered to their home by FedEx, and I would ask if they can look at some videos. Majority of the time, they say yes, and I'd give them the link (https://lp2.kb-universe.com/?referer=tbatcb1830). Then once they see it, they Facebook us at TEAM

BUTLER SAVE IN GOLD and say thanks because that was what they were looking for. My wife has made so many friends this way. I, on the other hand, am very cautious. For one, it's hard to get in my circle, and everyone is not for you, including other veterans. So I'm always on alert when I'm speaking to or meeting other people, I want to always stay in my lane and not belittle or disrespect other people's opinions.

Tatina and I continue to work on my claim. Reason being, here we go, I can't do it alone. I need a help mate now. I realize that women assist to soften our tone as we speak. This is another disability I fight with, but God put this man and woman of God in front of us, pastor and copastor and a host of others, that you will read about in the thank-you section. It's been a struggle as we pull from different ends as we start to put this over 3,159-page puzzle into order. My wife reminds me of the attorney in the wheelchair, Ironside, from that television show. Tatina dissect every piece of evidence as if she was a (CSI) crime scene investigator agent. Things in my report that I saw and thought I was doing something, comes behind me and dissects it to the third and fourth power. Well, statistics say two heads are better than one, who am I to complain. My wife and I have sent evidence to first lady, Michelle Obama and received one phone call, not from the first lady but from an aide. I guess the other information is still being looked at, and we will send another information packet out at the end of the month, which is the same information we faxed to the evidence intake center. We have a good feeling this will get first lady Obama and staff's attention. It would be a nice gesture if we could get an apology from the Secretary of Veterans Affairs, Congressman David Scott, Senator Johnny Isakson, the President and Vice President, in a letter or in person, to all of the veterans that got put in this messy situation. The Bible said closed mouths don't get fed, so I'm putting it out there. When God is on the seen, anything can happen.

Well, my case is coming up in 2019; like I stated, I'm on God's time and I'll continue to let *him* do what I couldn't.

CHAPTER 2

Who Can You Trust at the VA or Regional Office

If you want happiness for a lifetime—help someone else.

Veterans with post-traumatic anxiety issue experience the ill effects of a mixed bag of indications that meddle with their abilities to get delight from customary life, remarkably conditions that were constant, repetitive, or encased one or a ton of endeavors, can likewise be casualties of post-traumatic anxiety issue. Post-traumatic anxiety issue could come about once an individual endures an occurrence or situation that is outside the standard of customary mastery, surpasses the individual's saw capacity to fulfill its requests, and represents an overwhelming risk to the death toll.

Self-destructive veterans meet the formal criteria for post-traumatic anxiety issue. Serious and delayed risky torment isn't one thing that all soldiers and veterans endure. Veterans in perilous emergencies feel that they're at the snapping purpose of what they'll manage. Suicides of our veterans alongside relatives are on the ascent here in the United States; it's a condition that represents a substantial danger to the death toll, family, and groups. We have been remaining around considering self, as opposed to our neighbors who we see consistently however are so occupied it would be impossible to surrender a hand to the following. What happened to showing a man how to fish and he could nourish a town? I figure we're all wrapped up into ourselves until an issue or an inability or dis-straightforwardness thumps at your front entryway and now you require that hand up. Now is the right time to close the rotating entryways.

Numerous veterans, if not all, are frequented by memories of intense emergencies, demonstrations of mischief toward oneself, or broadened times of extreme dejection. Like soldiers going into ranges obscure, we tend to survive times of our time inside which we tend to have a sensible and persistent worry that we'd quickly be dead. Veterans tend to experience the ill effects of having been in risk, severally unequivocal injuries could have added to perilous presentation to the casualty of soldier or another person.

As of late, I have talked about the concerning vital in demonstrating this tension issue claim for VA administration joined preferences. In any case, acquiring the VA to recognize that this inadequacy is clarified to administration is just the essential fight inside the war to impel administration associated preferences. The clarification that you essentially petitioned administration joined remuneration is brought to your insufficiency to not get perceived for the inadequacy.

The way that the VA has organized the rating criteria is to remunerate veterans for the loss of gainfulness inside the workplace attributable to the veteran's administration associated inadequacy.

Odds are that on the off chance that you've got tension issue, it influences essential parts of your working capacity. Inside the few cases that different veterans concerned me with, nervousness issue has extremely influenced veterans' home life.

The VA has had an extended history of legitimately denying and under retribution tension issue administration associated cases. The VA has intense cases including maladies that they can't see or wherever they can't live it in "target" tests. Therefore, even once the VA recognizes that a veteran has uneasiness issue connected with administration, despite everything, they figure out how to belittle the veteran. The matter begins with the C&P exam.

There are numerous side effects that I see the VA disregard, moreover alluded to as drive administration. Uneasiness issue influences individual's capacity to subsume anxiety amid a customary way and for the most part winds up in veterans lashing out, hollering, or changing into vicious.

For reasons unknown, the VA does make a bad showing of talking about these indications inside the C&P exams for tension issue. My wife and I have found for my situation, these manifestations have been made light of or minimized and reported. As a veteran, the VA specialists are experts at under recording veterans and relative's concerns. Along these lines, if a specialist doesn't particularly raise worries about the veteran who has issues with resentment or roughness, the veteran isn't advancing to just let them know their worries. A lot of times I tell or my wife will tell the specialist our worries, and when we go get a duplicate of the subsequent notes, our worries are nowhere to be found. We feel disregarded, and I get upset like the other veterans and come weakened and distraught at times. Why go to a place that should aid you yet downplays your manifestations so you are denied benefits? While regardless they get a paycheck off of your hard work, I believe that is so unfeeling. How do you sleep at night knowing that you are putting God's children out on the streets in view of you would not do the right thing? I don't rest much, simply ask my wife.

As to the underneath recorded manifestations, in the wake of looking into C&P exams on administration associated nervousness issue, I'll let them know that the specialist noticed that the veteran didn't have any issues with resentment. The veteran can then tell the primary consideration doctor all the outrage issues that they told the specialist; anyway, it wasn't incorporated with the doctor's C&P report. I don't comprehend why this happens. The VA has structures that permit the specialist to place in notes, and in this manner, the VA has made their C&P inspectors perform heaps of exams accordingly, maybe they have next to zero time. Notwithstanding the reason could likewise be its fundamental that the veteran request and survey a copy of their claims document so they could audit the test.

So what are you ready to do to be prepared for a VA C&P test for a rating of administration associated disorder issue? It's fundamental that you bring some kind of records before the test, considering the outcomes that PTSD has on you. Audit the variables that VA uses to rate disorder issue. I may urge you to make a rundown of your uneasiness issue impactful to you. This may be hard to swallow, however it is essential to make positive that the doctor gets all the information that he or she needs to portray the right picture of your case. I also urge you to bring on a witness that is mindful of your tension issue. I would request that the specialist identify with this individual to get a fuller photo of the incapacity also.

Battle veterans, sex wrongdoing survivors, and diverse casualties of injury are inclined to a condition alluded to as Post-Traumatic Stress Disorder (PTSD). Veterans with post-traumatic anxiety issue experience the ill effects of a spread of manifestations that meddle with their abilities to their general customary life.

Individuals who endured harming toward one condition, altogether conditions that were ceaseless, repetitive, or encased may also be casualties of posttraumatic anxiety issue. Posttraumatic anxiety issue could come about when somebody endures an occurrence or situation that is outside the conventional skill, surpasses the individual's saw capacity to fulfill its requests, and represents an overwhelming risk to the death toll.

Suicidal veterans meet the formal criteria for post-traumatic anxiety issue. Serious and delayed perilous toward oneself agony isn't one thing that the larger part people endure. Veterans is unsafe toward oneself. Emergencies feel that they're at the edge of what they will manage. Approximately twenty thousand to thirty thousand people died by suicide every year inside the United States; it's a condition that represents an overwhelming risk to the death toll. The veterans administration is just presently starting to lead studies!

As I sit here writing, without end, my dissatisfactions about the foul play of our legislature, as I keep on reading more about my brothers and sisters in arms committing suicide and including their families truly exasperates me. Realizing that these administration representatives, doctors, and whoever else that we trust and utilize to maintain their expert obligations to general society has fizzled us appallingly and still gather a paycheck but tells us we're more concerned about pay than our disabilities. Well, our disabilities allow us a paycheck so that we can pay bills like everyone else. How could we do this to the groups of the Fallen Disabled Veterans of America? Why is nobody being arraigned and accused of tampering with proof? Are we that credulous, and do we truly mind what happens? Are the veterans not people? Why are we so affronted the best nation in the world with the best military with a high increment of self-destructive rates and vagrancy on the increment. Again I ask, how are you in government getting paid a check and getting paid forever when our veterans are in such a disorder? This is humiliating. How you can say you work for the veterans yet are the motivation behind why veterans confer suicide, are destitute, are divided from families, in what manner would you be able to adore yourself doing this which you know is so off base. This does not develop groups, families, and organizations. This pulverizes in the event that you took a financial aspect class. This does useful for nobody. On the off chance that your family or companion was requesting their benefits, I know you would verify; they get their benefits; you would walk them right on through, and I can say this on the grounds that I've heard it being carried out by representatives at distinctive VAs. An individual at the director's office and I were talking, and I said I know of veterans getting advantages for battle PTSD and never been in a combat area. That is not all, how would you get a combat infantry badge (CIB) while stateside and get benefits and that is not your (MOS) military occupational skills there, not taking a look at these records. These claims adjusters at the regional office, alongside the specialists and the C&P exam psychologist, need to have a body camera on and have a third-party organization screen all occasions. A significance organization can turn cameras on and off from a local area. There will be some stipulation that will oblige the camera use, yet we as Americans and disabled veterans require each one's help to get this camera laws with the goal to assist in the process of a veteran being treated and respected properly.

Integrity
Commitment
Advocacy
Respect
Excellence

My compensation and pension exam doctor was not going by the VA. I CARE motto. Follow me, I went into the office, and the doctor asked me if I am in school. I say yes for my bachelor's degree in business and administration. The doctor asked why, and I said it's because I have a house and two cars and that I did not want to be homeless again like I was in El Paso, Texas, twice in the same year. This doctor just put I am in school to attain a degree in business administration.

The same doctor wrote that I was boasting about my book, being on the news and doing book signings. I stated to the good doctor that I wrote my life story while at the University of Phoenix as a homework assignment, which is here in the VA hospital library, and that I am a veteran advocate. The doctor told me that I do not speak like I have PTSD. Question, how does someone with PTSD speak? This doctor used blogs and put into my medical records, which had a bad review of what I wrote in my book *PTSD My Story Please Listen*! But the doctor never went and put in what Huffington Post, ABC News, 11 Alive News, or CNN stated about me "Paying it Forward" or giving over three hundred free haircuts to the homeless veterans, veterans, and soldiers in my community. Just only the things to make the good doctor look good, again what does this have to do with PTSD? It's all right to fight a war. It's not all right to be human and care about another person's well-being and giving them free haircuts or going to a veterans meeting which the VA set-up. The VA sent me to school. There were no criteria that states if you have PTSD, you cannot attain a degree. There was nothing stating I could not write about my life. There was nothing stating that I could not do a book signing or be interviewed on the news or worldwide media. *But again, it's alright to fight a war.* The war gave us PTSD, why is it that the government is trying to save money off the backs of the warriors who fought for *freedom*! But third world countries get billions of US dollars? All this was is a smoke screen so that you cannot obtain your benefits or as I like to say doctors giving their personal opinions. Check this out, the doctor contacted the rater and told them I saw Mr. Butler on the news, and he has PTSD, what is his rating for PTSD? The rater went into my files, which I filed an appeal a few years ago and was awarded a favorable decision one hundred percent. Total and Permanent with Individual Unemployment. Later on, I filed for another disorder and the rater looked at my entire file. They looked at old evidence that was considered in the appeal and not only denied me the new disorder but reduced my other benefits too. This was based on their interpretation of evidence that was already interpreted /considered. Now, why didn't the good doctor, who cares for veterans put this information in my C-Files? A rater cannot overrule a favorable decision; I was told from higher up. I never gave consent to have my records reviewed, medical doctor or the QTC Exams, or Piedmont Henry Medical Hospital in Stockbridge, Georgia or Urgent Care and McDonough Family Care ever stated my migraines went from 50 percent to 10 percent. Welcome to the I CARE system! The VA and the regional office received all outside medical information that they asked for and overlooked vital information but still receive a paycheck to this day. I guess it's all right to get rewarded for robbing taxpayers and disabled veterans.

http://www.cnn.com/2015/09/02/politics/
va-inspector-general-report/

http://www.disabledveterans.org/2015/11/10/
veterans-affairs-caught-falsifying-doctors-qualifications/

http://www.kare11.com/news/investigations/
va-fighting-release-of-names-tied-to-brain-inju-
ry-exams_20160328053639187/105322210

http://www.military.com/daily-news/2016/04/16/ig-report-va-
has-been-shredding-documents.html#.VxUosaf9Zeg.facebook

http://www.militarytimes.com/story/veterans/2016/04/15/
va-employees-disciplined-health-enrollment-scandal/83091632/

http://www.sandiegouniontribune.com/news/2016/
mar/31/va-investigation-sandiego-waittime/

http://www.usatoday.com/story/news/pol-
itics/2016/02/24/111-va-medical-facili-
ties-flagged-investigation/80809426/

http://www.wrdw.com/home/headlines/Augusta-
VA-employee-charged-with-falsifying-medical-
records-316309411.html?device=phone&c=y

Veterans and soldiers, for your information, open 38 CFR,
Chapter 4, Subpart B and learn what you need to have a *successful*
claim. If not, you're doing yourself a great *injustice*. I would never tell
anyone the CFR is just for me. I'd rather teach a veteran so they can
teach another veteran. I can do it for them, but I'd rather teach veterans what I know. Self-help is encouraged and recommended. Any
veterans group can assist you, but veterans need to play a *proactive*
role in their claims. Therefore, learning what the CFR states is essential. If you teach yourself to fish, you will never go *hungry*!

http://www.benefits.va.gov/warms/bookc.asp

http://www.reviewjournal.com/chuck-n-baker/
veterans-who-suffer-ptsd-now-eligible-purple-heart

http://www.stripes.com/blogs/stripes-central/stripes-central-1.8040/army-clarifies-standards-for-awarding-of-purple-heart-for-mild-tbi-1.142250

http://www.usatoday.com/story/news/politics/2015/11/11/veterans-affairs-pays-142-million-bonuses-amid-scandals/75537586/

For a person to go this far, I feel that this was or is a personal attack on myself and family. I have contacted the media here in Atlanta, Georgia, along with Senator Johnny Isakson, my attorneys and pastor and copastor. This is why veterans commit suicide, on the grounds that raters and doctors taking things personal and voicing their opinions. You give them all the information needed, then your paperwork is held up for thirty days after calling, pleading, going into hardship. This is one of many reasons this system is failing our veterans.

My pastor called me and my wife since I'm the head of the house to the pulpit, and pastor told my wife to let it out, meaning all of what we were going through fighting this battle. My wife let out this cry that I never heard before, and it seemed like the women in the church followed her lead; it shook me. Pastor looked onto me and said you will live, and I repeated I will live since I was going to blow my brains out. My mind was racing but going nowhere. I will continue to pray for our government, and myself, and family.

CHAPTER 3

The Vet Center

Happiness consists of giving and serving others.

There are many agencies who welcome home war veterans with honor by providing quality readjustment during a caring manner. Vet centers perceive and appreciate veterans' war experiences whereas aiding them and their relations toward a productive post-war adjustment in or close to their communities.

Vet Center History

The vet center program was established by Congress in 1979 out from the mass Vietnam era vets returning home, who were still experiencing readjustment issues. Vet centers are community based and a part of the US department of veterans affairs. In the month of April 1991, in response to the Persian Gulf War, Congress extended the eligibility to veterans served throughout alternative periods of armed hostilities after the Vietnam era. Those alternative periods are known as Lebanon, Grenada, Panama, the Persian Gulf, Somalia, and Kosovo/Bosnia. In the month of October 1996, Congress extended the eligibility to incorporate WWII and Korean combat veterans. The goal of the vet center program is to supply a broad vary of content, outreach, and referral services to eligible veterans so as to assist them create a satisfying post-war readjustment to civilian life.

On April 1, 2003, the secretary of veterans affairs extended eligibility for vet center services to veterans of operation enduring freedom (OEF) and on June 25, 2003, vet center eligibility was extended to veterans of operation Iraqi freedom (OIF) and later operations inside the worldwide war on act of terrorism (GWOT). The relations of all veterans listed on top of are eligible for vet center services further. On August 5, 2003, VA Secretary Anthony J. Principi licensed vet centers to furnish sadness content services to living oldsters, spouses, youngsters, and siblings of service members UN agency die of any cause whereas on active duty to incorporate federally activated reserve and national guard personnel.

The good that I find at the Atlanta vet center and what they do for the veterans and their families is that when no one else listens to you, your voice when you are around other counselors and veterans and their spouses are being heard loud and clear. Everybody looks to one another as a resource as we all give off good information that could be useful to the next band of brothers that attend these meeting on the last Monday of the month. I told my C&P exam doctor that if they came to those meetings (the C&P doctors), they could learn a lot from the veterans' wives who deal with these disorders every day, not these one-time C&P exams that these doctors put what they feel on paper, and it becomes law. The look on her face was priceless. But hearing these women, not stories but testimonies, had other wives teary-eyed, and at one time, I passed tissues to a veteran's wife as a result of the pain was so etched in her bones, and the pain had been aching her for many years that she was in need of comfort from the group. That is what I find comfort; no one looks at you as crazy or as a number, or you do not get the feeling of being run in like cattle. The Atlanta vet center truly cares about their veterans and family and work hard to make sure that you and your family safety as well as the public safety is at hand. I also attend individual session which is more intense, but in some way, it helps with the devils dancing in my head and these horrible night terrors that haunt me, and now my family which they do not deserve, but my wife chose to say I do when we got married. Tatina is learning from these wonderful women, caregivers of these veterans, and she is soaking the knowledge up like a sponge and is working diligently to help me cope with my *disease* as my PTSD is starting to rub off on her as the other wives from their husbands.

Progress Note

April 15, 2014, Intake Note D: forty-six-year old married OIF vet referred by VAMC MHC for treatment of PTSD. Vet is hundred percent SC for IU. He reports sleep disturbance, intrusive thoughts, anxiety, irritability, and depression. Denies SI/HI at this time. A: Vet exhibiting all symptoms of PTSD. P: Begin weekly individual therapy to establish coping skills.

Progress Note

May 12, 2014, Individual Session D: vet continues to have daily intrusive thoughts, and they are creating problems in his daily activities. He states he is performing relaxation techniques although they are not diminishing ruminations. Vet is having problems concentrating to complete tasks due to these intrusive thoughts. A: PTSD chronic and severe. Vet is trying to accept and integrate the experience embedded in ruminations. Vet is not coping well with increase in intrusive thoughts of trauma. Vet presents alert, oriented, cooperative with poor eye contact. Speech was pressured at times, affect flat, and anxious mood. Thought process was organized with no paranoid ideation or systematized delusions. Vet has some impairment in attention and concentration. No A/V hallucinations or H/S ideations. Insight and judgment are poor. P: Continue weekly individual therapy to improve coping skills to control PTSD symptoms. Client will demonstrate increased success in utilizing coping mechanisms to reduce the total time in ruminations and reduce the degree of distress they engender. Vet to avoid and minimize the impact of ruminations.

Progress Note

June 16, 2014, Individual Session Therapy Note D: vet continues to report sleep disturbance with nightmares. Vet states he has been utilizing relaxation techniques and light exercise before retiring to no avail. Lack of sleep is very draining for him. A: PTSD chronic and severe. Vet continues to have trouble sleeping. Appears techniques to improve sleep patterns are not as effective as in the past. He presents with flat affect and depressed mood. He has fair insight and judgment. Speech was somewhat pressured, overly anxious, with marked impairment in concentration and attention. He was alert, oriented, and cooperative with poor eye contact. Thought process was organized with no paranoid ideations or systematized delusions. No HI/SI presented at this time. No audio/visual hallucinations observed during this session. P: Weekly individual therapy to improve coping skills and reduce symptoms of PTSD. Vet to continue a regimen of light exercise prior to his bedtime. He is to continue relaxation techniques learned. Vet report an increase in the number of hours of sleep.

Progress Note

June 30, 2014, Individual Session D: vet reports significant sleep disturbance with nightmares this past week. States at times feels out of control with irritability being a major negative issue. Wishes to control sleep patterns and reduce anger outburst. Vet is utilizing techniques learned to improve his coping skills. A: PTSD chronic and severe. Vet presents with flat affect and depressed mood. Speech mildly pressured at times. Vet was alert, oriented, and cooperative with fair eye contact. Thought process was organized with no paranoid ideations or systematized delusions. No active/visual hallucinations or H/S ideation. Significant impairment in attention and concentration. Insight and judgment are fair. P: Weekly individual therapy to assist in improving sleep patterns and reduce anger.

Progress Note

July 14, 2014, Individual Session D: vet reports constantly being on alert and very anxious this past week. Vet continues to be hyper vigilant, and he expressed problems this is creating for him. He reports an increase in daily intrusive thoughts and sleep difficulties. A: PTSD chronic and severe. Vet is trying to gain an understanding of the sources of his hyper vigilance. Vet presents with flat affect and depressed, overly anxious, with marked impairment in attention and concentration. Thought process was organized with no paranoid ideations or systematized delusions. No audio/visual hallucinations observed during this session. Vet has poor insight of judgment. No HI/SI presented at this time. P: Weekly individual therapy to reduce symptoms and improve coping skills. Vet demonstrates commitment to manage unwanted behaviors driven by his hyper vigilance.

Progress Note

August 4, 2014, Individual Session D: vet reports a detachment from family and friend during the past few weeks. He states he is isolating more, and there is no emotional investment to participate in activities. Vet wishes to identify new strategies to increase involvement with others. A: PTSD chronic and severe. Vet is having difficulty becoming involved in activities and involvement with others. Appears his coping skills are not as effective as they have been in the past. Vets presents alert, oriented, cooperative with poor eye contact. Speech was pressured; affect flat, and mood anxious. Thought process was organized with no paranoid ideation or systematized delusions. Vet has some impairment in attention and concentration. No A/V hallucinations or H/S ideation. Insight and judgment are poor. P: Continue weekly individual therapy to improve coping skills to control PTSD symptoms. Client will demonstrate increased success in utilizing coping mechanisms to increase social contacts outside of treatment.

Progress note

September 8, 2014, Individual Session D: vet attended scheduled appointment and updated on recent psychosocial stressors. He isolates at home and avoids interacting with others for fear of conflicts and confrontation. Vet continues to have periods of irritability which is negatively affecting relationships. Wishes to reduce isolation tendencies and eliminate stresses. A: PTSD chronic and severe. Vet continues to have difficulty controlling irritability. Vet presents in depressed mood with flat affect. He is alert, oriented, and cooperative with no paranoid ideations or systematized delusions. No audio/ visual hallucinations. Vet has marked impairment in attention and concentration. He has poor insight and judgment. No HI/SI presented at this time. P: Weekly individual therapy to reduce symptoms and improve coping skills. Decrease isolation tendencies to increase social contacts. Work on reducing irritability and anger.

Progress Note

September 22, 2014, Individual Session D: vet reports a detachment from family and friends during the past few weeks. He states he is isolating more, and there is no emotional investment to participate in activities. Vet wishes to identify new strategies to increase involvement with others. A: PTSD chronic and severe. Vet is having difficulty becoming involved in activities and involvement with others. Appears his coping skills are not as effective as they have been in the past. Vet presents alert, oriented, cooperative with poor eye contact. Speech was pressured; affect flat, and mood anxious. Thought process was organized with no paranoid ideation or systematized delusions. Vet has some impairment in attention and concentration. No A/V hallucinations or H/S ideation. Insight and judgment are poor. P: Continue weekly individual therapy to improve coping skills to control PTSD symptoms. Client will demonstrate increased success in utilizing coping mechanism to increase social contacts outside of treatment.

Progress Note

October 6, 2014, Individual Session D: vet continues to have difficulty controlling intrusive thoughts which are occurring on a daily basis. States this is affecting his ability to complete tasks. Coping mechanisms that have been successful to stop intrusive thoughts in the past are not working at this time. A: PTSD chronic and severe. Vet is working hard to control intrusive thoughts although not as successfully as in the past. Thought process was unorganized with paranoid ideation. Vet presents in depressed mood with flat affect. He is alert and oriented with poor eye contact. Speech was pressured at times and very anxious. No audio/visual hallucinations noticed during this session. No HI/SI presented at this time. P: Weekly individual therapy to reduce symptoms and improve coping skills. Vet to work on reducing intrusive thoughts and establish effective coping mechanism to control these thoughts.

Progress Note

November 17, 2014, Individual Session D: vet continues to have difficulty controlling intrusive thoughts which are occurring on a daily basis. States this is affecting his ability to complete tasks. Coping mechanisms that have been successful to stop intrusive thoughts in the past are not working at this time. A: PTSD chronic and severe. Vet is working hard to control intrusive thoughts although not as successfully as in the past. Thought process was unorganized with paranoid ideation. He is alert and oriented with poor eye contact. Speech was pressured at times and very anxious. No audio/visual hallucinations noticed during this session. No HI/SI presented at this time. P: Weekly individual therapy to reduce symptoms and improve coping skills. Vet to work on reducing intrusive thoughts and establish effective coping mechanism to control these thoughts.

Progress Note

December 1, 2014, Individual Session D: vet continues to have difficulty controlling intrusive thoughts this past week. This has interrupted his daily routine and states he is having difficulty employing coping self-statements, which has controlled intrusive thoughts in the past. A: PTSD chronic and severe. Vet is trying alternative techniques to cope with ruminations and reduce the degree of distress they engender. Vet presents with flat affect and depressed mood. He was alert, oriented, and cooperative with poor eye contact. Speech was pressured, overly anxious, with marked impairment in attention and concentration. Thought process was organized with no paranoid ideations or systematized delusions. No audio/visual hallucinations observed during this session. Vet has poor insight and judgment. No HI/SI presented at this time. P: Continue weekly individual therapy to reduce symptoms and improve coping skills. Vet demonstrates ability to utilize coping strategies to divert or extinguish intrusive memories.

December 8, 2014
Department of Veterans Affairs
Atlanta Regional Office
PO Box 100033
Decatur, Ga. 30031-7021
Dear Adjudication Officer:

Mr. Curtis Butler III xxx-xx-xxxx has been a client at the Atlanta Vet Center from April 15, 2014 to present receiving therapy for Post-Traumatic Stress Disorder directly related to his combat experience in Iraq during military service. He reports detachment from family and friends with significant patterns of isolation and withdrawal resulting in severe social impairment. Mr. Butler continues to experience sleep disturbance with nightmares, daily intrusive thoughts, daily panic attacks, flashbacks and high states of irritability which results in his inability to maintain employment.

Mr. Butler clearly meets all the diagnostic criteria for PTSD. Prognosis is poor and therapy will continue on a weekly basis to assist in controlling these chronic and severe symptoms.

Sincerely:

CHAPTER 4

The Different Men I Brought to the Bedroom

Happiness depends on you.

W hen taking as much as eighty-five different medicines prescribed to me from the veterans administration from 2007 to present, you have to wonder how you are going to act or respond once you take them. It's like going on a very slow roller coaster ride which picks up speed in a matter of seconds. You get a mixture of mood swings, depression, sadness, crying, and anger, suicidal, and homicidal tendency. Now, no one want to be around you but then again you need a babysitter just in case a family member has to call the police and rescue for help. I sometimes wonder what will kill me first, the disabilities or the meds which supposed to help manage my *disease*. When reading about the side effects which I receive a majority of them, it has myself and my wife very concerned. I always bring up that I will die before you Tatina and that I need to get my last will in order and to make sure that an autopsy is done on me.

Many of these side effects I do have, and as you continue to read in further chapters, you will read my personal medical reports, and you will also read about the many concerns my wife, my friend, and caregiver along with other veterans and spouses speak on the seriousness of said outcomes. I sometime wonder who the man in the mirror is. When I look in that mirror, I do not see Curtis Butler III, I see and feel a veteran, aging quickly from the inside out. These meds that are prescribed to me by the VA along with post-traumatic stress disorder, traumatic brain injury, migraines, other disabilities, and the list goes on and on as you will see in other chapters. It is wearing and tearing down on my body, mind, soul, and spirit. My wife is so stressed trying to cope and deal with my issues and *dis ease* when put together *disease*. It's driving her out of her mind, and this will make an ordinary woman break and leave. As I look at my situation, I would leave myself if I could, bringing these many men to our bedroom with my wife is ridiculous and is wrong, and Tatina does not deserve this. No wife or husband deserve this treatment. With this said, Tatina still looks over me as I cry uncontrollably and telling her I should have died in Iraq with my battle buddies, or that I want to go back to Iraq and be with my military family rather than being with my family at home. Again, I ask, who is Curtis Butler III? What did my wife see in me that I did not see in myself? I wonder if a wife or husband could love so many personalities which changes speed faster than a formula 1 race car driver during a race. These side effects are just as dangerous as our disabilities. It's basically like playing Russian roulette or rolling the dice in life. We have our ups and downs due to disabilities, and plenty of times, I just want to give up and blow my brains out or sit in the garage with my car running and door closed or driving off of an embankment. My body is used to the medicines I take, and it's doing me more harm than good. These are the dancing devils that follow me into the bedroom and in my everyday life. I'm up for days not sleeping; I take naps which last maybe two hours. I rather watch my wife, Tatina and daughter, Nia sleep and make sure they're all right. But I did not feel like my wife was acting like a wife. The majority of the time, my mind and think-ing is slow and cloudy almost as if it is standing still. Plenty of times I sit with a blank stare, and my wife would ask what I was thinking about. Sometimes it's nothing and other times I would wonder who Curtis Butler III is, or I think about my battle buddies not here hang-ing out with me like we have done on many occasions. After the side effects wear off, it's just as bad. It's like you're coming out of a very bad dream in slow motion, and you're trying to speed it up so that you could have some type of control of your body, soul, spirit, and mind. Every time I close my eyes and when I think I am going to get some good sleep, the night terrors take over, and I feel my body being tossed and turn which way as I am trying to wake up, like in the movie *A Nightmare on Elm Street*, and I see myself getting killed by the Iraqis every time on the missions that I went on. It has gotten so bad that I see soldiers that I used to know that are now resting in paradise when I am not sleeping.

CHAPTER 5

PTSD Does Not Mean You are Stupid

Happiness does not lie on happiness, but on your achievements.

PTSD is the normal reaction of a normal person to abnormal circumstances.

What is PTSD? PTSD may be a set of symptoms that surface once a very dangerous, scary, and uncontrollable traumatic event which occurred. PTSD has several causes. As a veteran, it's presumably the results of the experience of war. However, you are the victim of another traumatic event like a violent crime, accident, physical or sex crime, or a natural disaster. PTSD symptoms comprise four categories:

> AVOIDANCE—amnesia, disassociation, numbing, hyper vigilance, dominant behavior, and isolation.
> RELIVING—flashbacks, sleep disorders, overwhelming feelings, and overreacting
> VICTIMIZATION—distrust, abandonment, helplessness, concern of modification, blaming others...
> SHAME—feeling guilty, feeling as if you're crazy, feeling unworthy, feeling unwanted, and feeling hurt.

PTSD is the dancing devil in our head! The proof is mounting that anxiety disorder, notably chronic acute anxiety disorder, significantly changes the electrical and chemical reaction of the body on a permanent basis. This causes accrued probabilities of attack, strokes, and other long health issues for our veterans.

Going back to college with PTSD was scary for me. My anxiety level was up. I did not know if I would be accepted, and I felt different in uncharted waters. It took me seven years, but I finally will graduate with my BSB/A. I had an instructor who did a couple of radio interviews with me on KTEP Radio 88.5 FM in El Paso, Texas. The instructor mentioned that I was a difficult student and that we got through the class well, being he knew how to recognize when things are not right and to fix them the best way he knew possible. Stress and anxiety, for instance, are potential issues caused by environmental factors that affect the veteran's individual life. These could occur solely at times in response to stimuli. Though stress may be a natural part of school thus, all students could experience this difficult and nervous point in time or forthcoming an examination or PowerPoint presentation. These are the things I went through at the University of Phoenix in Santa Teresa, New Mexico, and Atlanta, Georgia. Generally, that stress could also be caused by one thing entirely outside the university setting and be one thing way more serious, like post-traumatic stress disorder.

Post-traumatic stress disorder is in a class characterized as anxiety to include behaviors and physiological responses that result when an exposure to a psychologically traumatic event. Symptoms will seem shortly when the event or generally months later, however to maneuver the identification from one amongst acute stress disorder to post-traumatic stress disorder, symptoms should persist for quite thirty days, and that they should produce difficulties in one or a lot of vital areas of life functions.

I read and heard that one of the foremost talked concerning causes of post-traumatic stress disorder nowadays is military service. Among veterans of the Iraq and Afghanistan wars, the rate of post-traumatic stress disorder is approximately 13 percent and will continue to rise. As a result of symptoms, it might not show up for months or perhaps years later, these numbers are expected to rise.

Among Vietnam war veterans, concerning 9 percent of men and 11 percent of women, had post-traumatic stress disorder at the time of a study conducted in the early 1980s, whereas more men and women had post-traumatic stress disorder following their time in Vietnam. This could have wide implications for the sector of upper education. With the passing of the Post-9/11 GI Bill, there has been a rise within the range of Iraq and Afghan war veterans attending school.

When it involves the school setting, post-traumatic stress disorder presents some terribly serious issues. For some veterans, it's going to be troublesome to be around individuals and to attend large classes, take exams in a full classroom, be registered full-time or as is common in combat veterans, dealing with the common noises and stimuli in a school setting. Also, the veterans with post-traumatic stress disorder usually have sleep disorder and depression, which can cause synchronous problems like the shortcoming to focus in school and maintain motivation. However, it's important to notice that post-traumatic stress disorder doesn't mean that these veterans have any less ability to stand out in their classes.

Accommodations are created to assist these veterans bring academic success. Disabled veterans are allowed to require online classes wherever attainable. The University of Phoenix allows you to turn individual assignments later. The accommodations rely upon individual circumstances and therefore the aspects of the trauma that has occurred.

11 Alive News in Atlanta, Georgia, did an interview on when my benefits were cut in half. As the reporter and I spoke, I informed him that the regional office and VA Hospital in Decatur, Georgia, told me the way I speak does not add up to me having PTSD. I told them PTSD does not make a man or woman stupid. We have disabilities that trigger different things. The reporter agreed and said that is ridiculous. When I was awarded to go back to school, I was never told that I could not get a degree from the VA or the education department at the regional office. My C&P exam doctor when asked what I going to school for, and I responded business administration. The doctor's response was, why? And I responded to her that I have

a house and cars and I'm trying to keep them. My reason was that I was homeless while in El Paso, Texas, twice in the same year. My next question is are these C&P doctors qualified in the PTSD field or do they just need a medical doctor behind their name? Why is there so much deceit at the VA hospital and regional office? The veterans maybe crazy in view of what we have done for *freedom*, but *PTSD does not mean you are stupid!* The veterans administration have a PTSD questionnaire which last approximately three hours. It all depends on the amount of question they give you. I had about 340-something questions, and it was, how are you with family members, how well do you do in a crowd, and a list of others, which in the eyes of most veterans is bias. PTSD is different in all veterans. There are no wrong or right answers. The questions should have asked how you heard about the soldier being killed or injured, how you feel being in harm's way, and approximately how many times you have come under attack or your unit. Again, we need to work together. The VA and regional offices, along with the president, vice president, the secretary of VA, and the congress, need to realize that we did not have PTSD, migraines, traumatic brain injuries, or any other disabilities before going on these suicide missions called war. Another suggestion that will assist the veterans is, if you've been in combat, all soldiers should receive a combat badge stamped on their DD Form 214. This will also help speed up the process for veterans receiving the right benefits whether you have or do not have a combat (MOS) military occupational skill.

Sometimes these symptoms don't surface for months or years after returning home. They will conjointly come back and go. If these issues won't go away or are becoming worse or you're feeling like they're disrupting your daily life, you might have anxiety disorder.

Some factors will increase the probability of a traumatic event resulting in anxiety disorder, such as:

- Being hurt by losing a brother or sister in arms
- The intensity of the trauma going on around you

- Being physically near the traumatic event
- Having an absence of support once the event occurred
- Feeling you weren't on top of things

A wide style of symptoms are also signs you're experiencing PTSD, such as:

- Feeling upset by things that prompt you of what happened
- Having night terrors, vivid reminiscences, or flashbacks of the event that cause you to desire it's happening everywhere once more
- Feeling detached from others
- Feeling numb or losing interest in stuff you accustomed regarding care of
- Becoming depressed
- Thinking that you're always in harm's way, scanning your surroundings
- Feeling anxious, jittery, or irritated
- Experiencing a way of panic that one thing dangerous is on the point of happen
- Having problem sleeping
- Having hassle keeping your mind on one issue
- Having a tough time with reference to and obtaining alongside your better half, family, or friends

"When stress brought on flashbacks, I would self-medicate with a fifth of an alcoholic drink to run away from life." It's not the symptoms of anxiety disorder however how you confront them which will disrupt your life. You may:

- Frequently avoid places or things that prompt you of what happened
- Consistent drinking or use of medicine to numb your feelings
- Consider harming yourself or others

- Start operating all the time to occupy your mind
- Pull away from people and become isolated

These are the things my wife and I go through on a daily basis every day. I pray that one day, I, Curtis Butler III could get off this roller coaster ride and to be normal again. To just be a regular citizen and pay my bills and take care of my family and to enjoy my new life.

Action Required: Faculty Notification of Services—MGT/488
Tuesday, April 21, 2015, 11:13AM
To: Instructor
Cc:ptsdmystorypleaselisten@yahoo.com

Hello, INSTRUCTOR,
Regarding: CURTIS BUTLER III and MGT/448

You have a student in your class with an approved classroom accommodation under the University ADA guidelines. Please read over the attached *Faculty Notification of Disability Services* and *Faculty Responsibilities—Americans with Disabilities Act (ADA)* forms and retain for your records, as they outline your responsibilities. **The Disability Services Office does <u>not</u> require a signed returned copy of the *Faculty Notification of Disability Services* form.**

All information pertaining to the student's accommodation/condition should remain confidential. Please contact me if you have any questions about the implementation of the accommodations described on the Faculty Notification of Disability Services Form.

If your student is receiving additional time to individual assignments (as indicated on the attached *Faculty Notification of Disability Services* form), please note the following:

Students receiving this accommodation have until the end of the course, plus the additional time indicated to submit individual assignments. For example, in a 5 weeks course, a student with 1.5 times the normal time to complete assignments will not be required to turn in assignments until four (4) days following the end of the course. **Please do not publish the student's final grade until all individual assignments and/or tests have been submitted or the student's extra time has passed**, unless notified the student will be taking an IX grade.

If the student needs additional time beyond agreed upon extra time after the course ends to submit any remaining individual assignments and/or tests, the student must request an IX grade from the Disability Service Advisor. In the event the student will be taking an IX grade, I will send a notice to you and the student with the IX deadline date. The IX grade differs from an I grade (Incomplete) in these areas:

o   IX grade will be given regardless of academic standing.
o   There is no automatic one letter grade deduction.
o   No Incomplete Grade Contract form is needed.

Individual assignments are defined as individual projects/papers due during class, including checkpoints. The additional time accommodation does not apply to learning team assignments, discussion questions, participation, or weekly summaries. (If the student is late on any of these requirements, your classroom grading policy will apply.)

Additional information can be found on the Faculty Resources & Publications page of eCampus, under "Guide to Student Disability Services." Thank you very much for your time, and please let me know if you have any questions.

*****

Disability Services Advisor

University of Phoenix
Disability Services Department
4025 S. Riverpoint Parkway, Phoenix, AZ 85040
Mail Stop: CF-S907
Phone:
Fax:
Email:
Assistive technology technical support call 866-842-5222.

Visit the Disability Services Page at http://www.phoenix.edu/students/disability-services.html

This is an example of how your paperwork should be presented when providing Statement In Support Of Claim VA FORM 21-4138 evidence to any of your service officers. Good luck and again thank you for your service.

STATEMENT IN SUPPORT OF CLAIM VA FORM 21-4138

The following statement is made in connection with a claim for benefits in the case of the above-name veteran:

On numerous occasions inside and outside the (FOB) Forward Operation Base (BIAP) Baghdad International Airport, I PFC Butler at the time worked on the General's Security Team, as well as in the office and around the (FOB). I also took pictures of incidents that happened on the (FOB). My primary (MOS) 92G10 a cook.

Incident 1) A Soldier was on the phone at the AT&T Center (I think that is what they called it) and a mortar round or rocket came in and hit nearby causing injury to a Soldier and damages to equipment and the ground.

Incident 2) We were attacked at approximately 0300. The reason I know this is because a Soldier and I were returning from the (MWR) Morale Welfare and Recreation tent playing pool. Soon as we entered our tent, all of a sudden air sucked the tent in and the pressure from the air popped the tent right back out. We heard a loud "BOOM" sound from a rocket. It hit four tents right where we had just walked. We were terrified! We relocated to our concrete bunkers until the all clear. I tossed and turned all night. Noises startled me throughout the night. If we had left 10 minutes later, we would have been killed. The SPC and I would have died that morning because it would have been a direct hit. It was even terrifying the next day when I had to go back and take pictures. This SPC saved my life because I was not ready to leave but he was tired, and we had to have a Battle Buddy at all time. One Soldier did get injured I think trying to outrun the shrapnel metal and ran into the porta john, and it went through the porta john and hit his leg.

Incident 3) A Soldier died of a Non-Combat action. We had just spoke less than 24 hours, and the next day, he was dead. I cried like I lost a son. This Soldier was on my mind, and I couldn't sleep. I kept seeing him in my sleep. The Soldier who was also a friend of mind was telling me something, but I kept jumping up out of my sleep.

Incident 4) A Command Sergeant Major (CSM) and his team got attacked with gunfire and Improvised Explosive Device (IED). The team came back shocked, confused, dazed and looked like they saw the devil themselves. A man, a giant, who was without words, let you know it was real when you left the Forward Operation Base (FOB), it was life or death. I was there when they returned and witnessed the account. Hell, I was scared because I never went outside the F.O.B., and I knew the next mission was going to be me and my team. I was scared as heck and went into the latrine by myself and cried in the stall.

Incident 5) I was told a SGT and SPC were walking to the MWR tent on 4 July 2003 when we were attacked by mortar and rocket rounds onto the FOB, shrapnel metal struck both Soldiers causing the SGT to be paralyzed and causing some disability in the SPC right arm. The SPC M-249 was bent like a pretzel. The SGT had shrapnel metal in the back of his head. I'm sad to say I just lost another "BROTHER IN ARMS," SGT passed in his sleep due to his injures on 4 July 2003, Baghdad.

Incident 6) CSM was not supposed to go off the FOB on 24 Dec 2003, but like all Soldiers, we want to rollout with our team. We are family; we're all we got when in the war zone. CSM said Merry Christmas to us and prepared to roll out with his team. Next thing I knew one of the HUMVEE got hit by and I.E.D. And CSM was (KIA) Killed in Action.

CHAPTER 6

Veterans and Family Members of Veterans Speak Out

The enemies of happiness are boredom and pain.

PTSD Statement

My name is Ms. S Curtis Butler and I were stationed together in Hanau, Germany, assigned to 2/501st Avn Bn. We were deployed to Baghdad, Iraq in April 2003–August 2004. We were mortared on a daily basis. We were attacked during the middle of the night and during the daylight hours. The mortaring was so intense that it had the whole compound nervous and jumpy. The slightest boom and everyone was running to the bunkers. We were all paranoid to some point; some more than others. Curtis Butler saw a little more action than most of us. He use to pull security for the General when he needed escort outside the compound. So, he did come under attack more than some of us. So, I'm sure it is quite disturbing at times for him with all the memories of the shooting and mortaring going on outside the compound as well as inside. (Wednesday, April 6, 2011)

Stressful Incident #1

It was approximately December 03, when Saddam Hussein was caught, and many Soldiers were celebrating our Victory when all of a sudden, we started to receive incoming. It was in the evening of that night between 1900 and 2000 hrs. Incoming in and around the Forward Operation Base (FOB). This was enough to make someone crazy and forget what to do next but run for cover. Myself, SSG P, and SPC Butler would run for cover and stay under cover until it all stop. SPC Butler would start complaining about headaches and even blackout from the headaches. He really was hurting that evening.

Stressful Incident #2

On July 4, 2004, at approximately 0100 hrs. SPC Butler returned from the Morale Welfare and Recreation (MWR) tent and which the same time we started receiving incoming again which resulted in one of the Soldiers receiving an injury from the rocket attack landing in our (FOB). The Soldier was leaving the porta potty (the outside bathroom) and was injured in one of his legs.

Stressful Incident #3

SPC Butler, myself, and many other Soldiers slept in the same tent in Baghdad International Airport (BIAP), SPC Butler would wake up yelling incoming and we all would roll over to the side of our bunks and take cover. I yell out to SPC Butler that's not incoming, but a vehicle or helicopters would be passing by. They sounded really loud and as if it was incoming. SPC Butler really was tripping over the sounds of incoming. I had to take him to the aid station numerous times for these reactions. I did believe that he had an issue that needed attention. SPC Butler really has a sleeping problem; he snores really loud and at times sounds like he stops breathing while sleeping. This is not a good thing; it could cause him to stop breathing and die. SPC Butler is a good Soldier and followed all orders given to him with no negative response.

Stressful Incident #4

Early evening of July 4, 2004, there was incoming in our FOB which resulted in a Non-Commissioned Officer (NCO) and a SPC injured from this attack, the NCO was paralyzed and the SPC had an injured arm and M-249 weapon destroyed. This had a great impact on SPC Butler; he knew the SPC very well and it affected him personally. It could had been any of us getting hurt.

Stressful Incident #5

One day when we were in the hangers in BIAP, I was on the second floor of the hanger, and SPC Butler was waiting for me on the bottom floor when I turned around and observed someone was on the ground in the middle of the hanger. I ran over to see who it was, and it was SPC Butler. Many Soldiers responded to the area and gave him first aid. SPC Butler passed out, and we transported him to the aid station. This is not the only time SPC Butler passed out but many times. SPC Butler was going through a rough time trying to coup with this issue. I really believe that SPC Butler had PTSD with much depression. Hoping for the best and fast recovery. (Friday, April 8, 2011)

*****

Memo For
Atlanta Veterans of Medical Affairs Regional Office
Subject: Mr. Curtis Butler III

On or about 8 January 2014, Mr. Curtis Butler III had some significant damage to his home that caused him to have a tremendous flashback from his tour during Operations Enduring and Iraqi Freedom. Because of this occurrence, I personally observed the Clayton County Police and the local Paramedics on site to retrieve Mr. Butler from his home and take him to the Piedmont Hospital at that time. Additionally, before the authorities could enter his home, I had to calm Curtis down and escort him out of the house. He did not have any recollection of the date, location, and other key events that was asked of him by the police and paramedics.

J E M
MAJ (RET) United States Army

I, Retired Command Sergeant Major (CSM) A. M am submitting the following statement in support of the VA Claims process for Mr. Curtis Butler III.

I served on active duty in the United States Army, leading Soldiers, for over 30 years before retiring on July 1, 2003. I am a combat veteran of Operation Desert Shield and Storm (ODS) and conducted military operations in Bosnia in support of Operation Joint Endeavor. I am married to a 27 year veteran who served in combat, in ODS and both; Operation Enduring Freedom (OEF) and Operation Iraqi Freedom (OIF). Most recently, having served as a Lockheed Martin Field Service Representative in the combat zones of Korea, Iraq, and Afghanistan, working with retired and active duty personnel, I am well acquainted with the symptoms of post-traumatic stress disorder (PTSD). I have annotated these facts up front in this statement to assure its readers that I can lay claim to personal and professional experiences with PTSD over a 30 year career of dealing with service members who suffer from it. Upon entering the Army at the end of the Vietnam War, I first became familiar with the symptoms of PTSD when it was called shell shock and battle fatigue syndrome describing the behavior of mentally unstable Vietnam Veterans returning home from war. Because I was concerned for Soldiers under my leadership with these issues, I personally sought appropriate PTSD information and knowledge and eventually became professionally trained by the United States Army, in my capacity as a senior leader, to recognize PTSD symptoms, to better ensure the safety of Soldiers specifically in my commands. As a five time First Sergeant, (inclusive of my ODS experience) and eventually a CSM, I was required to provide sound advice to senior enlisted leaders and officers (general, field grade, and below) regarding the professional assistance essential to maintain the mental health and stability of those Soldiers impacted by PTSD in and out of the combat zone.

I recognize the symptoms of PTSD and have been involved with enough Soldiers long enough to judge character and distinguish the differences between Soldiers true crisis and those who were or are malingerers, liars, and or good actors, with their own agendas. It is my opinion, based on my personal and professional experience that Curtis Butler III does suffer from PTSD and should be afforded the maximum benefit allowable for treatment of this disability to the highest degree available.

At approximately 02:45 in the morning of January 8, 2014, I was contacted by Mrs. Tatina Butler, the spouse of Retired Army Soldier and ODS/OEF/OIF veteran; Curtis Butler III. Mrs. Butler was concerned that her husband was having "another breakdown" and asked if I could assist her in "calming him down." I initially advised Mrs. Butler to contact a veteran crisis "hot-line" so that a working trained professional could have verbal contact through cell phone with Mr. Butler who was away from home, unwilling to listen to his spouse and driving his personal vehicle on Interstate 75 South, at the time she contacted me. I eventually found Mr. Butler on Interstate 75 South in his vehicle, which he had pulled over to the side of the interstate. Mr. Butler appeared to be agitated, angry, depressed, and emotionally unstable. He was preoccupied and unfocused and rapidly switched from mood to another. All of this behavior was out of character and unusual, based on previous contact and conversation I had with him before. As Mr. Butler was in no mental condition to drive, I drove him home. I could physically see that he was upset and recalling episodes of combat, based on our conversation on the way to his house. He referred to his home as the "combat zone." Mr. Butler's home had undergone significant damage during a storm. The visual effects of the storm damage, flooding, and extensive electrical and roof repairs in his home had caused him to have flashbacks, reliving what he saw and remembered during his time in the combat zone.

Upon arriving at Mr. Butler's residence, I could understand why certain memories were triggered. I saw pipes hanging out of portions of the ceiling; waterlogged walls with electrical wiring showing through, heavy leakage, water soaked pulled-up carpeting and chaos of tarpped repairs in progress. I could truly relate to how those conditions could trigger painful memories. It reminded me of some of the blown out, buildings I had gone through during ODS. Mr. Butler was also upset, angry, and ranting about uncooperative insurance companies and irresponsible contractors, relating their behavior to "bad leadership and training." I continued to talk to Mr. Butler and so did the veteran's crisis hot line representatives Mrs. Butler had contacted. When I thought Mr. Butler was no longer a threat to himself or his spouse and knew he had professional assistance, I left his home. Before 10:00 the next morning, however, Mr. Butler's symptoms "had escalated" according to his spouse, who contacted me again. She said she had to stop Mr. Butler from attempting to commit suicide by swallowing several amitriptyline pills which had been prescribed by his doctor for previous episodes of depression.

Mrs. Butler told me that the police were in their home as a result of the altercation. Apparently, they could see that Mr. Butler was combative but not mentally responsible for his actions. They called emergency medical service (EMS) to assist Mr. Butler. Mrs. Butler said she was concerned for her husband's safety, since the situation with the police was becoming tense before the EMS arrived. Since Mr. Butler had become combative and angrier, she said, she thought the police may have been threatened by Mr. Butler's "episode" even though he was unable to think clearly about his actions. Mrs. Butler had attempted to explain to the police that her husband was a veteran diagnosed with PTSD. Even though Mr. Butler was initially refusing to cooperate with police and EMS personnel upon their arrival, they realized he needed special medical care and possible hospitalization because of his mental state and got him to the emergency room of a local hospital. By the time I got back to Mr. Butler's home, he had agreed to go with the EMS to a local hospital where he was admitted and placed on suicide watch with guards. The hospital eventually had Mr. Butler transferred to an institution better equipped to deal with PTSD episodes. The institution's staff saw that Mr. Butler was in crisis and also found it necessary to admit him. On one occasion, I visited with Mr. Butler while he was under care. He seemed to be progressing from the break he had experienced and was learning to cope with the escalating symptoms of PTSD, with the help of the staff at that facility. He spent several days there until he was mentally stable enough to go home.

On April 21, 2014, I received another call from Mrs. Butler as my wife and I were in our personal vehicle, on the way home from an outing. Mrs. Butler said Mr. Butler was having a "melt down." I asked my wife to advise her to call a veteran's crisis center, and we asked if she needed us to come to their home. She said "yes," and we went to their residence. Mrs. Butler escorted us into the kitchen where Mr. Butler sat. When we asked him if he was alright, he began to sob. Mr. Butler was distraught, depressed, and frustrated with "the fact that the VA was attempting to decrease his disability benefits for his PTSD diagnosis." My wife and I advised Mr. Butler of his rights as a veteran. We stayed with Mr. Butler, informing him of available assistance and possible courses of actions he could take to overcome some of the hurdles he was experiencing in getting the assistance he needed. We talked to him until he regained his composure and started talking about the steps he would take to initiate his plans to get assistance. We reminded him and his wife, that it was alright to use every available asset at his disposal whenever he found himself in crisis and not to hesitate to call for professional assistance whenever he needed to do so.

I am writing this statement on behalf of Mr. Butler because I believe, based on my experiences and conversations with Mr. Butler and his spouse that he is suffering from PTSD. The symptoms I witnessed, could easily lead to tragedy should they go unchecked and or are temporarily and inappropriately managed. From what I witnessed Mr. Butler go through, coupled with the horrific accounts and outcomes of veterans in weekly news reports who were unable to get necessary assistance, Mr. Butler requires every resource available, private and or VA sponsored, to sustain good mental health, and therefore a good quality of life. This cannot happen without the highest disability award. Therefore, I respectfully request that Mr. Butler's 100% disability assessment for PTSD be reinstated to allow him the care he desperately needs.

Mr. Curtis Butler III

On or about 8 January 2014, Mr. Curtis Butler III had some significant damage to his home that caused him to have a tremendous flashback from his tour Operation Enduring Freedom and Operation Iraqi Freedom. Because of this occurrence, I personally observed the Clayton County Police and local Paramedics on site to retrieve Mr. Butler from his home and take him to the Piedmont Hospital at that time. Additionally, before the authorities could enter his home, I had to calm Curtis down and escort him out of the house. He did not have any recollection of the date, location and other key events that was asked of him by the police and paramedics.

Author of Mindfulness Meditation for PTSD, TBI, and Compassion Fatigue

Curtis Butler III, provides a spirited defense and riveting account of the continuing importance of PTSD awareness, education, and training through first-hand experience.

Curtis Butler III, is creating a new paradigm for veterans through the congruence of rigid reflection, community involvement, and integrated approach to veteran education and realization. What emerges through Curtis Butler III, story is a beautiful enclave of enhanced self-healing and empowerment.

M T D Entaprize Music Worldwide BMI Renaissance Media Group

As the son of a 20 year Army veteran I am sympathetic to the needs of service men and women during and especially after their service commitment is complete. We have to be aggressive about the care, whether it is short or long term, of people who give so much of themselves for those who can't or are unwilling to do military service. Since meeting Curtis Butler III, I've been made aware of the travesty that is perpetrated against veterans returning from the war zone by the VA. We've seen evidence of this by a recent 60 Minute story regarding the despicable treatment of veterans seeking medical treatment by the agency they were told to trust. I think it is a wonderful thing that Mr. Butler is doing to shed light on his own experience and affliction (PTSD). I also admire his ability to deal with these issues in an open manner. This demands a lot of courage to expose oneself in such a way and I commend him for it. If we as a nation are not willing to deal with the mental and overall health of those who selflessly serve this country, then I don't think we should ask people to do so.

*****

April 2, 2014
To Whom It May Concern,

Today I stand up proud for a Veteran, and I urge all El Pasoan's, Active military, Veterans and Colleagues at El Paso area to do the same. El Paso Fort Bliss is home to the 1ˢᵗ Armored Division with 34,218 Active Duty; 1,634 Reservist; 43,994 Family Members; 10,670 Civilians. Area Population: El Paso: 827,398 (www.militaryin-stallation.com:2014). For this reason, I would like to share a story about a veteran who has live here in El Paso and cried out for help and yet we refused to listen. Yes, this city, All American City (2010) with huge military presence, we have rejected, refused and ignored this wounded veteran. But no matter the circumstance this veteran has manage to survive to sharing his story. He has written a book in El Paso about his mental health issue title "PTSD My Story Please Listen" about how war disable him to separate himself mentally from real life and yet we have manage to criticize him and call him crazy. But as a Soldier he has not given up. He has attempted to talk to local news station (KFOX-El Paso), news (El Paso times), radio (KTEP) and speak to local VA counselors and has anyone listened? This Soldier has given so much not only to fight for our country freedom but safety. Did you know that this veteran while attempting to deal with is anguish here in El Paso he lost his house, mental wellness, healthcare, and career? And we yet again we turn away from him. Ironically as a veteran in worse places like dirt holes, and endure hard mental anguish like watched his military family die in his presence. Yet that did not stop him from fighting during that time. He gave up his home so that we could live in our homes, he went under fire to provide us a safe work environment. Please listen to his message by watching the following videos.

Yes, we I also am ashamed as his Friend, Advisor, Colleague, El Pasoan, and fellow American to admit that I have not truly listened. I learned so much from talking to him today 04/02/14 as he came back to visit El Paso. He said he was not mad at El Paso, people were simply not listening, so he decided to move but will always come back to his roots, in El Paso, TX. When I ask him what has made him strong to keep going, hardship after hardship, and disappointment after disappointment, and he said "I keep fighting as I did in war time I will keep passing ammunition to my Soldiers on the left and right side, while we are under fire and keep fighting this fight, if I stop, who will keep providing them ammunition..." I tried to hold my tears back, but I couldn't. I clearly visualized his purpose in life, to keep telling his story about PTSD so that other veterans, fellow veterans, survive this mental health issue, and assist before it's too late. His new mission is to turn his bad experience to good deeds, this is his calling most importantly to live in the ways of the Lord.

Sincerely,
G G

*****

EL PASO PLEASE HELP BY DONATING...
Let soldiers know they are not alone... HOOAH!

*****

May 8, 2014
Distinguished Professionals,

I would like to take a few moments to share my personal experience with a true "Man after GOD's own heart." This man is "full of compassion for others" with little to no regard for himself. He is one who is full of joy and desires those around him to be encouraged that "if GOD did it for me, He will do it for you as well." I, speaking of Curtis Butler III whom I have known through our M.E.N (Meeting Every Need) Ministry monthly meetings, "Kingdom Man" Disciple class, Holiday Outreach events and our Man Power Higher Living 2012 event.

I was introduce to Curtis in early 2012 during our M.E.N Ministry meetings and subsequent classes afterwards and had the opportunity to witness his love for GOD and the people of

GOD. Curtis has shared his story of dealing with the challenges of PTSD from his tour of duty in the Army that left him homeless but never allowed these challenges to limit his desire to serve others. Dealing with the pain and hardship that this condition can have upon an individual, Curtis relied on GOD, the brothers in our classes and other Army associates to keep him encouraged. This is a direct testament to the resolve that Curtis has developed that allows him to be a "Great" advocate for the Kingdom of GOD and those at Higher Living Christian Church.

He has been blessed to write a book (PTSD My Story Please Listen) that speaks to the test and trials that PTSD can imposes upon those impacted. He has been on numerous radio and television programs sharing his story so that others can be encourage from how GOD has brought him through. As the Bible states "we are blessed to be a blessing," and Curtis takes that to heart as he went to pay his local light bill and was moved to pay bills for others that went into thousands of dollars. This speaks to Curtis' heart to give to others what GOD has given to him.

Curtis has relied upon GOD to lead, guide, and order his steps to be an overcomer that others could be inspired by. This complete trust and reliance upon the GOD he serves, lead him to his beautiful and loving life partner Tatina Butler. She has been the "helpmate" that GOD has set aside for Curtis to form the "Butler Team" that now seeks to assist other veterans (through "Butler for Vets" 501(C) nonprofit organization) that have been left homeless and abandon after their service to this country. It has been a privilege and honor to have met Curtis, and

I continue to be excited about what GOD has done and will be doing in and through the "Butler Team."

For HIS Glory,
Elder H S

*****

Elder H S
Evangelism & Men Ministry
September 2, 2015
To Whom It May Concern:

In the number of years that I have known Curtis Butler he has been a gentleman, Scholar, husband, father, and friend. He has a heart of gold as he is always looking to help those who are less fortunate. His altruism speaks volumes along with his willingness to always lend a helping hand to a neighbor, friend, or even a complete stranger. Curtis is a rare breed, and the truth is that the world would be so much better if there were more men like him.

Sincerely,
W B

September 3, 2015
To Whom It May Concern:

I am writing this reference to Curtis Butler, a young man that I have grown fond of over the years. Later came to Germany, deployed to Baghdad, Iraq, in which the 1/501st Aviation Unit was already in the middle of deployment. I meet Curtis Butler after I arrived at BIAP, and he seems nice and all. He was always on the go and always spoke in passing, with a kind word. If you asked him something, he would always go out of his way to find out for you. I later left because I was injured and was MEDVAC backed to Landstuhl, Germany.

Back in 2008, I came back in contact with Curtis Butler on Face Book and later exchanged phone numbers. He called, and we had a long talk about how he struggled to come to where he is at now. Curtis told how he was in El Paso, Texas trying to get help from the Veterans Affairs. He told me through the process he was homeless and did not have food to eat. There were times that he did not know where his next meal was going to come from. During that time, I was going through my waiting period with the VA about my VA Disability claims myself. The hardship Curtis faced was just the beginning, not only did he help countless veterans through the process as well.

Since talking to Curtis Butler, he has endured a financial hardship because the VA has decreased his benefits. There were times I would call him and would sound all down because he was having a migraine attack, and he would have to talk to me later. There were times he posted on Face Book that he was in the Emergency Room with severe migraines. I can attest to that because I have frequent migraines as well that have me in bed hours at a time. There were a couple of times I have talked to Curtis, he would be all upset; I would have try to calm him down. He would tell me that he had a terrible dreams, and I could tell it altered his thinking. (PTSD) Post Traumatic Stress Disorder was really getting to him because he would pour out his heart to me. I would just let him vent and then he would soon calm down. I would talk to him another day, and he would be to his senses. He would be laughing and joking with me and telling me he was getting ready to help veterans at the VA, helping them through their claims process.

I know these last past couple of months that Curtis has been really trying hard to get back his benefits. I know having a family, it can get stressful, when you are getting a certain amount of benefits. All of a sudden, they decrease your benefits without warning or letters mailed to you inquiring about the decrease. I would want to know why myself if there was a permanent decision made on my, behave of my illness or injuries.

Very Respectfully,
A R W

*****

September 5, 2015
To Whom It May Concern:

I remember as a teenage Curtis was there to help me when my father was at work. Gave me advice on lesson of life and took time to show me how to be a man. My dad and him would hang out on the weekends and have a blast. Curtis moved in with us a couple months later; he has an awesome personality, cheerful, loving, and a sense of humor. He always look for a chance to play with us or share stories. Always had that go get it attitude even challenge my brother and I to a weight lifting contest. After living with us for a while, Curtis start to sell his furniture and when I ask why he is selling his furniture, he told me he need money and choose to join the Army. I am proud to say that I am proud of the accomplishments he has done, and he set the path of me joining the navy and give it my all.

Sincerely,
A T S

September 5, 2015
To Whom It May Concern:

I SGT W (RET) joined July 06, 1989–mid September and went through Basic Training at Ft. Jackson S.C. with then PVT Butler. He was a young, high speed energetic Soldier. Took direction, did so well, in fact was made into a leader, himself. Leading a squad in Basic Training. Under a high level stress. Operating under a tempo most people who were just recently a civilian would not be used to, did very well. He could laugh and joke with the Drill Sergeants. Something of an uncommon thing. This is how I could remember him through time, so many years later. As not too many people can do such a thing, joke, and banter with the Drills. Almost unheard of back then. I had lost touch with him after that but later learned he was also stationed in Germany.

I now re-enlisted shortly after 9/11. Well, apparently so did he answer the call to duty? I met up with him in a reclassification (MOS) Military Occupational Skills at Ft. Lee, VA. Here again, he had been the same guy if not more so looking after his fellow Soldiers. Cheering them on for PT test even running back to pace someone or whatever else the cause in the field portion. He was a Soldier who lived the "same fight mentality." And even though he was not a (NCO) Non-Commissioned Officer at the time was still acting and displaying leadership qualities. For a Specialist, he would have been in my opinion "amongst the best" if I were to rate him at that time as a NCO in May/June 2003. I hope this gives a good insight and explanation to the Soldier I had known and served with in the time frames I served with him.

Regards,
SGT W J R (RET)

*****

September 8, 2015
To Whom It May Concern:

I've known Curtis Butler III since 2010 when we were classmates at University of Phoenix (Santa Teresa, NM). Butler had problems with basic instructions that were given by the instructor; it seemed as if his brain would just pause for a moment until he could process the information. We were in small groups, so he was able to take his time and contribute to the group and complete his class assignments—he has always been a fighter. I knew of Butler's migraines and knew that he was on medication to treat the episodes that plagued him.

I never knew that Butler was homeless while he was attending UOP, recently seen You-Tube accounts of his good deeds and accomplishments in his life, so it's great to see that he has finally finished his degree and not let his disorders and life issues keep him from obtaining anything he sets his mind to. I pray that they assist this young man, who has much determination and such a big heart.

Sincerely,
J W

*****

September 8, 2015
To Whom It May Concern:

This letter is intended as a character reference for Curtis Butler on behalf of J W S. I have known Mr. Butler for 30+ years since we were kids. We met in Charleston, SC due to our grandparents living on the same street. He was from NY. so some of his actions and ideas were different from our Southern views. As a kid I didn't understand, but now that I am a Navy Veteran, a former government contractor, and currently a skilled civilian worker (Senior Electronics Engineering Technician), I can put the pieces of the missing puzzle together. Curtis was simply exposed to a different life by living in NY than I, down South. During my working career, I have met many individuals that grew up differently than I, and it's been great for my growth. I am proud to say that Curtis began my journey of embracing those outside of my community and comfort zone as a kid, which has opened my eyes and life to incredible experiences. Curtis has and continues to expose me to different facets of life. Curtis has a huge heart, is generous with his time, and is a motivated individual. This can all be proven through his career in the military and his time afterwards. Curtis Butler is a good friend of mine from childhood that continues to keep in contact to impart and share life's experiences.

V/R
J W S

*****

September 8, 2015
To the Bravest Man I Know!

Curtis, my military big brother; I too have known this man for a long time. He is compassionate, honest, caring, and yet and still he has a dark side that no one should ever dare to encounter. Why you ask? Because of the service connected injuries, both physical and mental. I too suffer from depression and PTSD, and we often speak on how the U.S. Govt. has forgotten about us: us being the ones who bravely risked our lives for the love of our fellow men and our country. But now after he has given all that he can, he's left half the person he once was with horrid nightmares and images no one could imagine. Now when he needs the help from the Government, he receives constant rejection and now he has to fight all over again. Sadly, enough the fight is from the same Government as before… But Curtis and many other are the enemy. Now we must still fight just to live a substandard way of life. Why you ask? Because of our bravery to protect those who couldn't protect themselves. But who is going to protect us was well as Curtis from the constant denials, rejection, and mistreatment of us by the Govt. The Veterans Administration. We deserve better. I love my big brother Curtis Butler III, I will fight alongside of you in the trenches for justice, respect, and compensation for all that we have lost while serving our country! Thanks for nothing! We'll never give up or in! We will continue to fight for rights that should be given, after all, haven't we gave enough?

Butler was assigned to the General Security Team, and always treated Soldiers with a kind word, if he didn't know something, he would go get the answer and return. He also took pictures of incidents on Baghdad International Airport (BIAP) when we got attacked by mortar rounds and rockets. Butler also spoke of bodies of insurgents, the smell of the dead bodies and the condition that they were in. This was off the (FOB) Forward Operation Base, while going from one location to another. Butler had buddies that died and received horrid injuries. I'm not a doctor but war has affected us more ways than one. Butler was a little excited going off into the city, because his group or team was going out to do a job, to protect the people of Iraq and the base. Butler wasn't the sharpest but he knew security. He had to interview for that position with CSM. Yes, Butler is a cook, but he never cook while on the front line nor in theatre meaning Iraq. If Butler made mistakes or said anything wrong, I know him to be apologetic and sympathetic. Look what he is doing for his Military brothers and sisters not to mention other disabled veterans. PTSD does not make you stupid, if it did then a whole lot of us would be stupid, wouldn't you say? This man probably went to more funerals than any civilians I know. Butler has a big heart and sometimes he put his foot in his mouth, but surely everyone does from time to time. So is he the only one in the military that has done this? If so he should be a millionaire because no one on this earth is perfect.

Mr. Butler, you will always be a Hero in this life and the next. May God bless you today, tomorrow and always!

HOOAH!
D T

*****

September 9, 2015
To Whom It May Concern:

I have known Butler for 20 years, and he has never lived with me, he had his own place, I never spoke with anyone from the VA Hospital in El Paso, Texas or Atlanta, GA so I do not know where they got he lived off of me. I am the mother of Shamar, Adrionna and Brionna Butler when Butler was living in Kansas City, Missouri, he stayed downtown and I lived in Grandview. So that Dr. has falsified, slander and tarnished his name in his medical records which made my kids father look bad so that he could not receive his benefits which helps take care of his kids and which helps to make him homeless. I have no other words; I'm disgusted.

Sincerely,
V W

*****

September 9, 2015
To Whom It May Concern:

I have been a mentor and SGT to Butler in Baghdad, Iraq, and Germany from 2002 to 2006, Butler always went above and beyond the call of duty. When working security for the General, Butler's duties where security on and off the base, example when building tent city, Butler was in charge of 250 Iraqi Nationals, and on other days, Butler would do security as a driver or a gunner for Non Commissioned Officers, and Officers. They would call for him by name as stated in his ARCOM.

Butler had security duties of varies dignitaries and celebrities that entered the FOB from the President, Secretary of State, Race car driver, Sports Model and Congressional personnel.

Butler went out so much that we pulled him back, Butler was not pleased because as he said it his team is rolling out, and he didn't want to be left behind. Butler knows security and Soldiers he went out with knew it and trusted him with their life as much as Butler trusted them with his life.

We had Soldiers that got injured on the 4th of July that Butler knew, he was torn up inside and was a wreck talking in his sleep and jumping out of his sleep. We had a Soldier who huffed and died, and Butler's response was in a battle, my response was no huffing. Butler broke down and cried and said all he wanted was a beer a buzz, I just spoke to him and said first rounds on me when we get back Germany.

Butler has great leadership abilities even when people didn't show love, he kept it moving and said play time is over we have a job to do and focus on getting the job done by all means necessary.

Butler also had blackouts and very bad migraines which sent him off the (FOB) Forward Operation Base to the hospital in order to be treated and was on bed rest. Whether we got attacked or not, I knew it was getting serious because Butler had to get shots for these attacks. Butler has fallen out in the hanger due to migraine and taken to the aide station on numerous occasions.

When Butler left Germany returning to the States he had 13 or 14 ribbons and awards on his uniform for cooking and awards in the battlefield and the most coins in his unit. Butler's cooking awards came from competition and during training. I'm not a doctor but you just don't get those by being anti-social.

I'm proud to know this young man; he even finish his Bachelors which took him 7 years with disabilities, mental and physical with being denied benefits and homeless, false statements from a Dr., statements off a blog which taints a veterans record, reduced of pay and benefits.

Sincerely,
(Ret) SSG G P

*****

September 9, 2015
To Whom It May Concern:

Curtis Butler III has to be one of the most selfless people I have had the pleasure of crossing life paths with. At the time I met, we both were renting rooms at an Extended Stay Motel in Norcross, GA. He actually was my next-door neighbor. Anyway, we eventually introduced ourselves and as the old saying goes, the rest is history. I really considered this man a friend and a brother. I even call him "Big bro" sometimes when I call. He is what I call a doer. If he says he's going to do something, he does it. Period. An honorable and honest man to say the least. His work to help veterans not just cope or survive with PTSD, but it shows how to live with PTSD. I mean really live life and enjoy it as it should be. And not feel stigmatized by the label of a "mental disorder."

I had the pleasure of doing the photography and video work for him at his first haircut give away. That day will always be ingrained in my memory because how many young men, single mothers, and veterans he helped that day. He's a good man, and I feel he deserves all good fortune that is coming to him for all the good he has done.

Thanks,
M T D

*****

September 9, 2015
To Whom It May Concern:

I have known Butler since 1986 when he came down from Brooklyn, New York, to Charleston, South Carolina, to visit his mother and siblings who resided on Martin Luther King. Dr. Butler introduced himself to everyone in the neighborhood, and we all took to him as if he grew up with us or as a family. Butler would go back and forth to visit his grandparents and cousins on Able Street because we all went to school and partied together and went to games together. Butler was like a big brother since he was getting ready to go into the Army, he would watch after us and ask what you want to do when you graduate, what are your goals, and if you didn't have one, he would ask why.

During Hurricane Hugo, Butler sent his entire Basic Training check home to his mom so that the family could have food, water, and a generator. Even though he was little boy when he went with his grandparents, someone taught Butler morals and how to lead by example. This is what people love about him and well sometimes try to take advantage of his kindness, because of his big heart. Butler doesn't know how to say no, because GOD never said NO.

When Butler returned from Iraq, he's more aggressive and watching every bodies move, and you can't walk up on him or he will snap and go off. He says he doesn't sleep much, and the VA gives plenty of medicine which he says doesn't help but makes him feel worse and useless.

Butler always tells me he should have died with his friends because they're not going through the hell the government is putting his fellow brothers and sisters in arms through.

Sincerely,

L S

*****

September 9, 2015
To whom it may concern:

I've known Curtis Butler III since 1984 while attending Thomas Jefferson H.S., in Brooklyn, East New York. I was in his home-room class, and Butler always had a smile on his face and was liked by students and faculty members. Butler was an A B student; he played on the baseball team at the high school and had a part time job. Butler was well mannered and always had something nice to say whether you were in a good mood or not. Butler took extra classes so that he could graduate quicker, meaning he took

12th grade classes in the 11th grade and would of graduated in 1985 but had only one class so he graduated in 1986 with myself and others. I also lived a couple of blocks from Butler and outside of school, still a nice guy to be around.

Once, we lost contact after graduating, I found him on classmate.com and then Face Book. This was like 2007 Butler was living in El Paso, Texas stationed at Ft. Bliss Texas. Butler was having issues with his benefits there and was tired of going to one hospital and mental hospital after the other. Butler said he felt like a Guinee pig taking different pills that bloated him and made him feel worse than before, with different mood swings and not liking him or others. I told him that I spoke with one of my Soldiers, and they told me to tell Butler that they will help him here in Georgia. Butler was also going through a homeless time which he could not get Social Security, disability benefits, or food stamps. They told him he made too much. Butler benefits then was 50% approximately $789; he has suicide attempts and didn't have family there and was lost in a Veteran system that did not care.

When I was getting ready to deploy to the war zone, Butler told me of the dangers to look out for, like they would booby trap dead bodies and animals, and not to pick up anything you did not drop or place on the ground; it could be explosives. Butler told me of Soldiers he spoke with and then later found out that they were killed, died, or were injured, spoke of the different memorials he went to. Butler told me of the migraines due to explosions and rocket attacks on the (FOB) Forward Operation Base. Butler said it would be worse when it's a full moon because the enemy can see your every move like it was day time. Butler would tell me it was exciting because of the adrenaline rush when you know you're going out with a kick-ass team to go get the bad guys or deliver important information to the green zone where the Iraqi dignitaries are housed and protected by US forces and their allies.

Butler spoke to me about the lack of sleep because of the attacks on the (FOB) and the sounds that sound like incoming and rolling over and telling Soldiers in the tent incoming when it was either a vehicle or an aircraft. I can attest to this because I went through everything Butler is speaking about in Afghanistan.

Butler has changed from his high school days, and war does that to you when people are dying and things blowing up around you; you leave the states with all your Soldiers and then come back home with less Soldiers and the things that we see that is not normal plays on our mental state of mind as well. Our lives are forever changed.

When arriving here, Butler asked if he could use my address so that he could receive mail because he stated that the VA said he could not use a P.O.B. at no time I spoke to a VA representative telling them that Butler resided at my residence.

(Retired) SFC A A

*****

April 22, 2016
To Whom It May Concern:

I'm writing this letter on behalf of my cousin Curtis Butler III. I have known Curtis all of my life as he is one year older than me. We have always had a special bond. We both lived with our grandparents in Charleston, South Carolina back in 1980s. Able Street was a dead-end street, so the neighborhood was close like family. All the kids grown up and played together, and all the parents knew each other. Some of us still keep up with each other. When Curtis came to live with us, he fitted right in with everyone. He would go to the different neighbor houses and made sure everyone was alright and made sure they didn't need anything. He would sit for hours and just talk to the older parents who were actually our grandparent's age. They would talk about any and everything that was on their minds. The older folks loved that he would take the time out to sit with them and help them out. He made them feel really special. He always had good heart and loved to help people. He is still like that to this day. I'm sure you have heard of the many things he has done to help other. He is a lot like my grandmother. She was the same way. This is one of the things I admire about Curtis, his willingness to help other. He was never afraid to talk to anyone. He would even hold conversation with strangers on the street. You don't find people like that these days. Everyone is just worried about themselves. Even though we don't talk every day, we do talk often to make sure everything is alright with each other and our families. I thank God for my cousin and his caring spirit. There are not a lot of people who will go out their way to help others, but he is one of them. I'm very proud of Curtis.

Sincerely,
M F

*****

STATEMENT OF SUPPORT OF CLAIM
April 22, 2016
Re: Curtis Butler III

The above-named, Curtis Butler III is my nephew, and I write to support him in his claim for VA Disability Benefits.

My nephew has been a part of a loving and nurturing family all of his life, and he has never exhibited the symptoms he has now until he went to the war zone twice in service to his country. Curtis lived with his paternal grandparents and when his father married, he lived with his father and stepmother until the two of them separated. He has been loved and cared for by his aunts, and he has lived on his own during his adult life after finishing high school. He has always been able to work and be involved in positive relationships.

Our family is close, but we are not perfect, and we are no different from the average American family. Prior to Iraq, Curtis was fine. While he was in Iraq, it became clear to all of us that he was in great distress and fearful due to the violence around him. His fear for his safety was intense, and we were very worried about him.

While in Iraq, he was always so happy to have a few minutes to call and speak to his family, and we were often worried about his state of mind and of course, his personal safety.

Curtis was depressed and distraught after his return from the war zone to the extent that he was hospitalized in June of 2007. We felt that it might have been a suicide attempt. In September 2007, I visited him for one week in El Paso, and he was trying to put on a good face, but I was aware of his feelings of fear, and he suffered severe migraines and insomnia.

Due to family support and encouragement, Curtis was able to try and focus himself by enrolling in college. His migraines and outbursts of anger continued, and he was encouraged to join a church. His attendance at church helped a little, but the psychological strains were still evident in some of his outbursts and his talk about things that happened in Iraq. The migraines continued.

He is a veteran who served his time and was badly damaged by the experiences in Iraq. No one can imagine what it feels like to be in that situation. Every veteran who is disabled is different. There is no "one-size fits all." The benefits that he deserves should not be in question. His care is the responsibility of the Department of Veterans and his compensation should not be denied.

Mrs. E B A

CHAPTER 7

God, Can we Talk?

Happiness can be found once all the distraction are gone.

First, I just want to say thank you, Lord, for blessing me when I was not in my right mind and for your continued forgiveness. Clean this house, Lord, and make me whole and complete; I yearn to be a better husband, father, brother, son, cousin, friend, and Christian man. Put people in our lives, Lord, who are for us and not there to waste our time and energy and take up space and air. We ask for people with giving souls who do not mind helping out mankind, whether going into the community and assisting homeless veterans, feeding, clothing, or just ministering to their needs. I know, Lord, you put my wife and I here for a reason, and we want to use our gifts for your glory, not ours. Seeing when you bless us, no man can take away; when you forgive us, it's a done deal. Thank you, Lord, for not being of the world as we know it today, where people do not forgive and who will run you over in a New York minute. You are the greatest man I know, and I want more and more of you, Lord. When I speak to you, you always listen and give an answer, always at the right time, which makes you an on-time God. I'm just in awe of your presence, and I know when you touch the president on down to everyone in his cabinet and show them the light and the right way to take care of Gods' people, we will be better as a society. Thank you, Lord, for the prayers of our government and this can also be used by anyone, and we can learn from *his* words. Thank you, Lord, for being the head of my household, and I apologize for being impatient when I already dropped you a letter in your inbox, which also stated I will take care at my time, so go out and enjoy life and breath the air and look at the scenery that I placed for you. I know in my families' future, Lord, things will be turning around for us. Thank you, Lord, for my pastor and copastor who calls and pray and listens to my hurt and disabilities of the world as the tears well in my eyes until it flowed like a river. Lord, I told the storm to go away so that my family could now have peace; we want peace from all of the disabilities I have endured from these past wars. Lord, I know you see the best in me when others look down on me as if I was the lowest piece of trash. At first, I was bitter, but now I'm learning to love me and the disabilities which is part of my resume. I raised my right hand twice, Lord, to defend the country and world that you made for us to love and enjoy. I find it therapeutic conversing with you for one, you do not judge or point a finger to scold me. Thank you, Lord, for your love, guidance, and understanding. Thank you also for having me as the founder of veterans lead, nonprofit. Thanks to my board member representative, El-Mahdi Holly and his dad, aka Uncle Tim for the name. Our motto, "Taking Veterans off the Streets One City Block At A Time." Now, I pray that you send me the right Christian people to run this organization and who are a hundred percent what veterans lead is all about. I pray, Lord, that the VA, along with the regional office, stop playing games with veterans lives because we matter.

1. VA, stop asking us questions about how we grew up to determine our disorder
2. VA, stop putting false information on documents that could end up in court
3. VA, stop and listen to the veterans and stop trying to use trickery in order to give the veterans a less than favorable decision
4. VA, stop with your opinions and go with medical terminology to determine disabilities

5. VA, stop comparing civilian PTSD with Combat PTSD; that's a slap in the face on both sides
6. VA, stop trying to take over the conversation; you were not there
7. VA, stop telling your patients to come off of unemployability in order to pay bills. You just told your patient to commit fraud, which is federal jail time, loss of the little wages receiving, penalties and fines, and paying the government monies received. Thanks, Doc. You're the best!

Prayer Confession for Justice and Peace

Praying for our Government

O, Lord, our God, the most-high God, maker of heaven and earth; our creator, our provider, and our protector. You are the just judge of all the earth, sitting on your throne of justice and judgment in the high court of Heaven. You, Lord, execute righteousness and justice for all who are oppressed. You are the Lord of the Sabbath, ruler of all, the God of angelic armies, fight against our enemies and avenger of our adversaries. Besides you, there is no Savior. Salvation is only of the Lord. Because of your great love toward all mankind and your love for justice and judgment, you said you will not forsake the saints but come to our aid on earth to uphold the justice upon which your throne in heaven and your kingdom on earth rests.

O Lord, bring your righteous judgment upon all those who walk in hatred and bigotry. Stretch forth thy hand and execute vengeance and recompense against all those who oppose peace and reconciliation. We know that Satan is behind every evil work that transpires in the earth. So we cancel his works now in Jesus' name. All violence, injustice, discrimination, suffering, humiliation, shame, embarrassment, loss, entrapment, sickness, and attacks are under our feet.

We ask that you execute upon them the judgment written, delivering us out of every affliction. Restore to us everything that has been stolen from us and our ancestors; everything delayed, bring it forth, now in this season. We command the release of inventions, opportunities, discoveries, businesses, industries, creative ideas, relationships, contracts, awards, inheritance and increase that have been fraudulently held up, misdirected, sabotaged, blocked, stolen, and destroyed.

We ask that you will give wisdom and guidance to all those who serve in place of authority in this nation. We pray for the president, the White House, senators, governors, mayors, commissioners, city council and all law enforcement officials. We pray that your love and compassion for humanity will reign in their hearts as they carry out the duties of their office. We ask that you strike down those who oppose justice, peace, and harmony in our land. Allow your peace to reign even in the political landscape of this nation.

We cast our eyes on the destitute, the poor, and the wronged, as we choose to follow you. We will preach good news to the poor, proclaim release for those wrongly imprisoned, and recovery of sight for the blind. We will set at liberty those who are opposed and proclaim the time of your blessing. Open our eyes to the downtrodden. Fill us with compassion for the plight of the alien, the refugee, and the immigrant. Lead us into ministries that help orphans and widows. Give us courage to block the paths of the ungodly who exploit the poor. So may your justice roll down like waters and your righteousness like an ever-flowing stream. Lead our footsteps to stand with the poor, which we might stand with you.

Execute your vengeance against the enemy speedily and bring to us the full recompense that is due to us as redeemed heirs of God and joint heirs with Christ that we may advance your Kingdom among men and nations. In the name of Jesus, amen.

CHAPTER 8

Denied is Not a Bad Word

"Happiness is a formula for courage"

W hen the regional office denies your claim, it can be real upsetting after going through such a traumatic experience event of a war or many wars. I have been denied four or five times, and I continue to fight seeing I have that right to take care of my family, and I'm not letting anyone tell me I cannot. When being interviewed by a counselor, ask questions and take notes, not everyone at the VA or regional office are bad apples; it's just challenging staying with that good one as they move you around so much which can be frustrating. Make sure you understand the words coming out of your counselors' mouth and ask to repeat. I feel for the counselors since they are over worked and have to see a certain amount of veterans, so at times, they may be as stressful as you are. I can say this by reason of I've spoken to plenty of veteran employees who work or use to work these areas, and I felt like buying them a drink and giving them a hug. Be business at all times, even when it gets tough. Give them as much proof possible from soldiers in your unit, a spouse, friends, coworkers, or family members describing in details how you have changed since returning home and what you have been through during the war. Know the different forms to put information on. In my case, the doctor put information on the wrong form, and it got returned back to sender. You would figure they would know, but no one in the office caught the problem. veteran buddy of mine caught it, and we fixed it. Remember to never give up. Someone will help you in your time and need. I found the veteran service officers a really good resource, and they went step by step with me and showed me what was wrong and how to fix it. Don't feel embarrassed to ask for help; this does not make you less of a man or woman. See, a lot of organizations do not show you how to fix it; they scan your paperwork then stamp it and send it on its way. This is one way how paperworks get backlogged and then chaos begins. If we learn to help one another out, much could be done to stop veterans from disliking the VA or regional office. Let us work together and help one another out for the better of all mankind.

This is an example of how your paperwork should be presented when providing *new and material evidence* to any of your service officers. Good luck and again thank you for your service.

Disabled American Veteran
Decatur, Georgia
RE: REQUEST FOR RECONSIDERATION BASED ON NEW AND MATERIAL EVIDENCE

I am requesting a motion for reconsideration of my claim for service-connected PTSD and migraines based on new and material evidence. I am requesting that my claim be re-adjudicated. Veterans and family members please DOCUMENT. DOCUMENT. DOCUMENT. And follow instructions from beginning to end. The evidence contained herein include:
Letter from Licensed Psychiatrist—includes confirmation of full access to documented medical history
VA Form 21-4138—Statement of Support of Claim-Submitted by Curtis Butler III

Department of Veterans Affairs-Atlanta Vet Center Records of Weekly Sessions

Recommendation for Award, dated April 25, 2004, Recommended Award: ARCOM

Department of the Army, Army Commendation Medal, dated August 15, 2004 for exceptionally meritorious service in support of Operation Iraqi Freedom

VA Form 21-4138—Statement of Support of Claim—Submitted by Tatina Butler, Spouse

Migraine Log—Maintained and Updated by Tatina Butler, Spouse

Record of 911 Call (Communications Event Report), dated August 9, 2014

Piedmont Hospital Record, dated August 9, 2014

Sincerely,

Curtis' sleeping patterns are very disruptive. He talks, cries, and makes threats in his sleep. Often times, he awakens soaked and wet. When I ask him about his dreams, he says he died and other Soldiers in his unit got killed in a rocket blast in Baghdad, Iraq. Sometimes, he tells me they are killed by an IED. He sees dead bodies in his sleep. He stays up watching TV all night at times considering he doesn't want to go to sleep as a result of the nightmares the night before. After nightmares and when he has been without sleep, his safety consciousness is heightened. He talks about bringing his guns to the home. If the alarm is not on or the doors of the house is not locked, he becomes very angry. He constantly checks the doors and windows during the night for safety. Also, during these times, his thought process is not logical. He is irritable, anxious, moody, detached, unaffectionate, very difficult to get along with, and avoids civilians—treats my daughter and I like the enemy in the "war zone."

Some of the things that Curtis avoids include: war movies (reminders of Soldiers in his unit getting killed in the war zone), movie theaters (it puts him in a panic state, reminder of the dark nights in the war zone), celebrations on Christmas Eve and Christmas Day (reminder of Sergeant Major death-has a migraine every Christmas and flashbacks), funerals of military friends (the playing of taps starts the migraines, dead bodies is a reminder of the war zone), sitting with his back to the door (he sits facing the door for safety-to-see who is coming in), military base memorials (reminder of Soldiers that died in the war zone), etc.

Resembles of an IED or the war zone equates to major problems. For example, the pipes burst in our home and there was a lot of debris from the burst. He said it looked like the war zone in Baghdad and that the busted pipe looked like an IED. He ended up on suicide watch and in a mental hospital (Pine Woods) for five days. Once when driving, a pebble hit the car front window. He became startled and I almost lost control of the car. He told me he thought it was an IED.

Signature Date Signed
Address Daytime/ Evening phone numbers

This is the aftermath after an (I.E.D.)
Improvise Explosive Device goes off.

I was assigned to the M-249 and 50 Cal while on
guard duty at the front gate in Talafar, Iraq.

Approximately 0800 or 8 A.M. a car bomb goes off in the Green Zone and leaves a crater in the road.

Mortar round hit outside Soldiers sleeping quarters, and blew out the ac unit.

Porta John which is our bathroom across from the tent was stuck by sharp metal. A Soldier received injuries. This is the inside.

We just got attacked in the afternoon on BIAP airstrip, pieces of the rocket was still in there.

Parts of the tent caught fire, thank God the
Soldiers where working that night.

This is the after math of the Soldiers
sleeping quarters after the explosion.

The same Porta John hit with sharp
metal went through the door.

This is the hole outside the tent where it hit.

Curtis Butler III convoy directions coming on to B.I.A.P

Going out on a mission in Baghdad, Iraq 2

Going out on a mission in Baghdad, Iraq

Home Sweet Home (B.I.A.P.) Baghdad
International Airport

Military weaponry destroyed parts of Saddam's palace

Military weaponry destroyed parts of Saddam's palace2

wedding cake

wedding bands

The McCleod and Butler Family along with Sandra
Maid of Honor and Albert Best Man

The Anthony's of the World Famous_THISISITBBQ

Tatina, Elder. Dr. Bliss who officiated the ceremony and I

Son and Dad and Veterans

Tatina Butler with her AKA Sisters

Nichelle Ponder Praise dancing to
the song_I Told The Storm

Me giving my Mom a kiss

Grandma McKay 102 years young

CHAPTER 9

Inspirational Quotes and Sayings

In order to have great happiness you have to have great pain and unhappiness otherwise how would you know when you're happy?
—Leslie Caron

1) I'm just human, I have weakness, I make mistakes, and I experience sadness; but I learn from all of these things to make me a better person.
2) Sometimes GOD doesn't change your situation because HE is trying to change your heart.
3) Until GOD opens the next door for you, praise HIM any way and anywhere.
4) Everyone is REAL until a real situation shows up.
5) I told GOD to protect me from my enemies, and I started losing friends.
6) When the past calls, let it go to voice mail. It has nothing new to say. (IG)
7) The struggle is worth the benefits.
8) People come and go. The only one that remains is you. Get to know that person.
9) Associate yourself with people of good quality, for it is better to be alone than in bad company.
10) Practice plus passion equals progress.

11) Be careful who you tell your business to; not everybody cares. And be careful who you share your happiness with; not everyone is happy for you.
12) I didn't come here to lose.
13) Train like a champion for the greatest sport of all—LIFE.
14) Stop waiting to be who you really are.
15) Never judge someone by the opinion of another.
16) Anytime a negative thought comes into your mind, change your perspective.
17) Fear is a LIE.
18) Remember GOD is the driver, so stop grabbing the steering wheel.
19) Earned, not given.
20) You messed up yesterday, but you'll mess up more if you let yesterday's mistake sabotage today's attitude. God's mercies are new every morning. Receive them.
21) If you want to fly, you have to give up the stuff that weighs you down.
22) A lesson will repeat itself until learned.
23) Relax. Breathe. Trust. Nothing gets away that is meant to be yours.
24) The only thing worse than going blind is having sight and no vision.
25) Five things to tell yourself each day: be positive and believe in yourself.
    • Today will be my day.
    • I am the best me there is.
    • I know that I'm a winner.
    • I can do it, I know I can.
    • GOD will always be with me.

CHAPTER 10

Migraine

I can do all things through Christ who strengthens me.
—Philippians 4:13 (NKJV)

Headache is regularly portrayed as a throbbing migraine commonly influencing one side of the head or face. In the event that you get headaches, however, you realize that there's a considerable measure more to a headache assault than simply head torment. Headache scenes commonly last no less than eight hours, with a great number people having side effects for an entire day. The headache comprises of indications happening before head torment, obnoxious side effects happening amid the season of head agony, and manifestations after head torment has determined. Side effects happening in every stage can add to the incapacity of headache.

The key time of a cerebral pain is known as the prodrome. These are signs that happen around twelve to twenty-four hours before head misery begins. Around one in three people with migraine will experience a prodrome. Standard prodrome reactions include: changes in attitude (like prickliness, bliss, or hyperactivity), digestive issues (like sustenance goals or free guts), neck desolation, yawning, and neurologic evidences (like wooziness, darkened vision, and issues concentrating). You or your family or allies may begin to see these movements to help anticipate drawing nearer attacks. Using migraine drugs in the midst of the prodrome can help check or diminish the earnestness of the horrifying bit of a cerebral pain strike.

A quality is a transitory unsettling influence of nerve capacity that for the most part starts around thirty to sixty minutes prior to the agonizing period of headache and keeps going a couple of minutes to sixty minutes. Around ten to twenty percent of individuals with headache encounter an atmosphere? Regular air indications incorporate changes in vision (like seeing blazing lights, crisscross lines, or blind sides), deadness on one side of the body, or disarray. In individuals more than forty years of age, an emanation once in a while happens without resulting head torment. A few individuals have atmospheres before some headache scenes yet not others. It's critical to see your specialist if your quality manifestations change or you build up another air.

In the midst of the horrifying bit of cerebral pain, you apparently have more unpalatable signs than basically head torment. People habitually experience affectability to reliably vibes that are not customarily unbearable, like fragrances, lights, and hullabaloos. People furthermore develop an affectability to touch, called allodynia. Allodynia portrays touch that would normally not be troublesome as anguish. A valid example, you may find it harms to wear a head band, your glasses, or studs in the midst of a cerebral pain. Brushing your hair may hurt. It may even hurt to have articles of clothing touching your skin or people touching you. Allodynia is a fundamental indication to search for. Investigation exhibits that some cerebral pain meds, as sumatriptan, are all the more effective when controlled before allodynia begins.

Once the troublesome bit of migraine has decided, you might regardless have reactions. This is known as the postdrome and impacts around three in every four people with cerebral pain. The postdrome continues going two or three hours to a day and is here and there depicted as a "headache eventual outcome." People routinely feel depleted, experience issues considering, and experience smooth waiting torment.

Making sense of how to see most of the times of your cerebral pain helps you better appreciate your evidences and plan treatment. If you have a postponed prodrome or air stage, you may have the ability to use fruitful non-sedate medications (like loosening up, bio-feedback, or exercises) or migraine medications to help treat early and grow your shots of avoiding a great, anguishing stage. Checking for allodynia can in like manner help perceive the best time to begin treatment. In spite of the way that the compelling torment time of a migraine is over, you may even now experience unpalatable indications that can interfere with your gainfulness called the postdrome.

Curtis Butler III
VA File Number xxx xx xxxxx
Tatina Butler's Record of Migraines

I, Tatina Butler, wife of Curtis Butler III, hereby submit my log of Curtis Butler III migraines.

September 2013—Did not maintain log of migraines

September 14, 2013—Piedmont Henry Hospital-migraine

October 2013—Did not maintain log of migraines

November 2013—Did not maintain log of migraines

December 22, 2013—Migraine

December 23, 2013—Migraine

December 24, 2013—Immobile, in bed with migraine this evening, complaining of throbbing pain, soreness

December 25, 2013—Do not want to be around anyone including me. He says he hates his life.

Piedmont Henry Hospital—migraine, flashback from Sergeant Major death Christmas Eve

December 26, 2013—Immobile, in bed from lingering effects of migraine headache (complaining of soreness, throbbing pain, sensitivity to lights and sounds).

January 1, 2014—Migraine

January 6, 2014—Migraine

January 7, 2014—Migraine

January 8, 2014—Tried to commit suicide, flashbacks of Baghdad, Piedmont Henry Hospital, sent to Pine Wood Mental

January 9, 2014—Confined to Pine Woods Mental

January 10, 2014—Confined to Pine Woods Mental

January 11, 2014—Confined to Pine Woods Mental

January 12, 2014—Confined to Pine Woods Mental

January 13, 2014—Released from Pine Woods Mental

February 14, 2014—Immobile, in bed with migraine this evening (complaining of pounding)

February 15, 2014—Immobile, in bed with migraine (complaining of throbbing pain, soreness, sounds)

February 21, 2014—Migraine

February 22, 2014—Immobile, in bed with migraine (complaining of throbbing pain on left side of head, sensitivity to sounds)

March 6, 2014—Migraine

March19, 2014—Immobile, in bed with migraine (complaining of throbbing pain on left side of the head, soreness)

March 26, 2014—Migraine

March 27, 2014—Immobile, in bed with migraine (complaining of throbbing pain, sounds)

April 8, 2014—Immobile, in bed with migraine this evening—it's very late, very moody, complaining of painful headache

May 15, 2014—Immobile, in bed this evening, severe migraine, death in the family

May 16, 2014—Immobile, in bed with migraine, complaining of pounding

May 20, 2014—Migraine

May 21, 2014—Migraine

May 22, 2014—During the playing of taps at Uncle Tony's funeral, migraine, could not drive car back to hotel, in bed from migraine rest of the day. Up and functioning later this evening

June 3, 2014—Migraine

June 4, 2014—Missed class today, migraine severe, went to VA Hospital

June 5, 2014—Immobile, in bed with migraine (lingering effects of migraine, soreness, throbbing pain)

June 8, 2014—Daughter's birthday today, immobile, in bed with migraine, complaining of pounding on left side of head

July 3, 2014—Migraine

July 4, 2014—Do not want to celebrate the 4th of July. Said it's not a day to celebrate when two Soldiers got injured today, a SGT and SPC

Immobile, in bed with migraine this evening-very moody, complaining of throbbing pain, soreness

August 7, 2014—Migraine

August 8, 2014—Migraine

August 9, 2014—Piedmont Henry Hospital-migraine, very moody

August 10, 2014—Immobile, in bed from lingering effects of migraine headache (complaining of soreness, throbbing pain)

September 1, 2014—Immobile, in bed with migraine, complaining of throbbing pain, soreness, extremely moody

September 2, 2014—Migraine

September 11, 2014—Immobile, in bed with migraine this evening-complaining of throbbing pain on the left side of head, sounds

September 12, 2014—Migraine

October 19, 2014—Migraine

October 20, 2014—Immobile, in bed with migraine this evening (complaining of throbbing pain, soreness)

October 21, 2014—Migraine

November 11, 2014—Immobile, in bed with migraine this evening-it's late, extremely moody

November 12, 2014—Immobile, in bed and migraine lingers with soreness, throbbing pain, sensitivity to light and sounds

November 20, 2014—Migraine

November 21, 2014—Immobile, in bed with migraine for part of the day (9a.m. to about noon)

November 26, 2014—Migraine

November 27, 2014—Immobile, in bed with migraine this evening, complaining of pounding

November 28, 2014—Immobile, in bed with migraine, complaining of throbbing pain, soreness

December 5, 2014—Immobile, in bed with migraine this evening, complaining of throbbing pain

December 6, 2014—Immobile, in bed with migraine until 2 p.m., complaining of pounding

December 7, 2014—Immobile, in bed with migraine this evening, complaining of pounding

December 8, 2014—Immobile, in bed with migraine this afternoon, complaining of throbbing pain

December 9, 2014—Immobile, in bed with migraine, complaining of throbbing pain

December 12, 2014—Immobile, in bed with migraine, complaining of throbbing pain

December 25, 2014—Immobile this evening, in bed with migraine

December 26, 2014—Immobile all day, in bed with migraine

December 27, 2014—Immobile all day, in bed with migraine

January 7, 2015—Immobile, in bed with migraine, noon until the next morning

January 8, 2015—Immobile, in bed with migraine, all day and night. Missed class

January 9, 2015—Immobile, in bed with migraine, all day

January 29, 2015—Migraine, in bed most of the day

January 30, 2015—Migraine, in bed most of the day

January 31, 2015—Migraine, in bed most of the day

February 2, 2015—Immobile, in bed with migraine from 1 p.m. until the next morning at 6 a.m.

February 13, 2015—Piedmont Henry Hospital, 11:28 a.m., Immobile, in bed with migraine, after returning home from hospital at 3:00 p.m. until the next morning

February 14, 2015—Immobile, in bed with migraine, all day

February 24, 2015—Immobile, in bed with migraine, this afternoon until the next morning

February 25, 2015—Immobile, in bed with migraine in the morning until transported to Piedmont Henry Hospital around 3 Released to Riverwood Behavioral Health, in Riverdale, GA around 11p.m.

February 26, 2015 to March 3, 2015—Committed to Riverwood Behavioral Health, in Riverdale, GA

March 23, 2015—Immobile, in bed with migraine until the next morning

March 24, 2015—Immobile, in bed with migraine, until the afternoon

March 29, 2015—Immobile, in bed with migraine, this evening

March 30, 2015—Immobile, in bed with migraine, until the afternoon

April 17, 2015—Immobile, in bed with migraine in the morning until the evening

April 18, 2015—Migraine

April 19, 2015—Migraine

April 20, 2015—Migraine

April 21, 2015—Immobile, in bed with migraine around 11 a.m. to the next morning

April 22, 2015—Immobile, in bed with migraine, around 10 a.m. until about 6

April 23, 2015—Immobile, in bed with migraine, this morning until about 2

April 24, 2015—Migraine

April 25, 2015—Migraine

April 26, 2015—Migraine

April 27, 2015—Migraine

April 28, 2015—Immobile, in bed with migraine until taken to urgent care. Went to Family Medical and Urgent Care in McDonough, GA at 6:45 p.m. Given a Demerol shot for the migraine.

April 29, 2015—Woke up with a migraine. Immobile, in bed with migraine until taken to urgent care. Went to Family Medical and Urgent Care in McDonough, GA at 6:30 p.m. Given a Demerol shot for the migraine.

May 5, 2015—Immobile all day, in bed with migraine

May 6, 2015—Immobile all day, in bed with migraine

May 7, 2015—Immobile all day, in bed with migraine

May 8, 2015—Immobile all day, in bed with migraine

May 16, 2015—Immobile, in bed with migraine this evening, complaining of pounding

May 17, 2015—Immobile, in bed with migraine this evening, complaining of pounding

May 18, 2015—Immobile, in bed with migraine this evening, complaining of pounding

May 28, 2015—Migraine, in bed most of the day

May 29, 2015—Migraine, in bed most of the day

May 30, 2015—Migraine, in bed most of the day

June 9, 2015—Immobile, in bed with migraine (complaining of throbbing pain, soreness, sounds)

June 10, 2015—Immobile, in bed with migraine (complaining of throbbing pain, soreness, sounds)

June 11, 2015—Immobile, in bed with migraine (complaining of throbbing pain, soreness, sounds)

June 12, 2015—Immobile, in bed with migraine (complaining of throbbing pain, soreness, sounds)

June 13, 2015—Immobile, in bed with migraine (complaining of throbbing pain, soreness, sounds)

June 18, 2015—Migraine

June 19, 2015—Migraine

June 20, 2015—Migraine

July 2, 2015—Migraine

July 3, 2015—Migraine

July 7, 2015—Migraine

July 8, 2015—Migraine

July 9, 2015—Migraine

July 20, 2015—Migraine, in bed most of the day

July 21, 2015—Migraine, in bed most of the day

July 22, 2015—Migraine, in bed most of the day

July 23, 2015—Migraine, in bed most of the day

July 26, 2015—Migraine, in bed most of the day

July 27, 2015—Migraine, in bed most of the day

July 28, 2015—Migraine, in bed most of the day

July 29, 2015—Migraine, in bed most of the day

July 30, 2015—Migraine, in bed most of the day

NOTE: This log should be read in conjunction with my Form 41-4138 which provides more descriptive details of how the migraines affect Curtis Butler III.

Please contact the undersigned at (000) 000-0000), if additional information is needed or for questions. You may also contact me at ptsdmystorypleaselisten@yahoo.com.

I certify that the statements contain in this document are true and correct to the best of my knowledge and belief.

Signature Date Signed

This is an example of how your paperwork should be presented when providing Statement in Support of Claim VA FORM 21-4138 evidence to any of your service officers. Good luck and again thank you for your service.

STATEMENT IN SUPPORT OF CLAIM VA FORM 21-4138

The following statement is made in connection with a claim for benefits in the case of the above-name veteran:

I, Tatina Butler, the wife of Curtis Butler III, hereby submit my statement on what I have personally observed about Curtis Butler III. The following is just a few of my observations:

Curtis has 8 or more migraines a month (see the attached log). When Curtis has a severe migraine, he becomes immobile. He complains of pounding or throbbing pain on the left side of his head. He is confined to the bed with no lights, no TV for 8 or more hours. It hurts to perform simple functions such as brushing his teeth. Talking to him is prohibited during these times. The sound of voices hurts; even his own voice hurts. Often times he tries to sleep through it but sometimes, he is awaken from his sleep due to the pain. We were told by Piedmont Henry Hospital he can only get a shot for migraines once a month. Also, getting frequent shots (once every month) would cause long term damage to his kidneys. To this end, he tries to avoid going to the hospital. On the days his migraine is not severe enough for him to be confined to the bed for 8 or more hours, the sound of his voice hurts, his speech is slow, it's hard for him to concentrate, and his thought process is illogical. On these days, he is confined to the bed for 3 to 4 hours.

CHAPTER 11

Coping Skills that Get me through the Day

There is nothing wrong with change if it's
going in the right direction.

1. Take frozen food out of the refrigerator and hold it in your hand.
2. Look up into the heavens and try to guest the forms and shapes of the clouds.
3. Perform a random act of kindness.
4. Look at pictures of vacation places or pictures of family and friends.
5. Write (letters, poems, journal, a book, or a song).
6. Paint.
7. Clean your home or car.
8. Pray.
9. Go for a nice drive.
10. Listen to some relaxing music.
11. Do schoolwork.
12. Go for a walk or run.
13. Take a hot shower or a relaxing bubble bath.
14. Light some candles and meditate.
15. Paint or draw.
16. Cook a nice meal.

17. Go to the park and feed the birds, ducks, or squirrels.
18. Talk to your therapist or hotline crisis center.
19. Read your Bible.
20. Read a good book.
21. Watch or go play your favorite sport.
22. Go watch your team play.
23. Go to a positive friend or family member's house.
24. Rearrange your furniture in your home.
25. Go get a massage.
26. Go get a manicure and pedicure.
27. Build something.
28. Take up a new hobby.
29. Chat on social media.
30. Watch your favorite television show.
31. Text or call a buddy.
32. Simplify your life.
33. Locate helpful groups.
34. Structure your time.
35. Do not make important decisions when you are feeling eerie.
36. Get a haircut or a different hairdo.
37. Breathe.
38. Go fishing.
39. Go to church or wherever you worship.
40. Plan an event.
41. Make a short- or long-term list of goals.
42. Stop blaming yourself.
43. Get or give a hug to someone.
44. Go horseback riding.
45. Take a power nap.
46. Make a smoothie.
47. Learn to play an instrument.
48. Look at your dream home or car or both.

CHAPTER 12

The Director's Office

The best apology is changed behavior.

As my wife and I go in and out of the veterans hospital corridors from one location to another, we finally end up at the Pete Wheeler Auditorium on the fourth Saturday of the month. I stated my concerns which involved deformation of character by a comprehension and pension doctor, to include a personal attack on my family and I. The new director spoke with my wife and I to lets us know putting blogs in a veteran's record is not acceptable, and that once you're a hundred percent total and permanent with individual unemployability the records was to be sealed, but it was not so. I also spoke with other veteran service officers, disabled American veterans, veterans of foreign war as well as my chapter at the American legion and everyone was on cue, except the regional office and VA in Decatur, Georgia. I have to say this new director wasn't pleased, and her team was helping me get things back to order. This book will probably be out before my benefits along with my twenty-five months back pay be reinstated. The director and her staff knew about this incident along with the head board of veterans affairs (B.V.A.), and still nothing to take care of this unjust. My wife and I are also asking for the license of this doctor to be pulled because you have to wonder how many other veterans and family members this has happen to. This is not how the I CARE System works along with Title 38 Federal Rules and Regulations. I ask that the VA, along with the raters, receive a block of instructions on these critical and important tasks at hand in order to cut down on backlogs of veterans' benefits. Your personal feelings do not have any rights at all in a veteran's medical record or falsifying statements, only medical terminology. These are some of the problems plaguing the VA and running up the taxpayers' dollars on redundant practices that hurt veterans as well as the community as a whole. We have to start somewhere, and Rome was not built in a day, but if we can get these two entities on the same track, we can make big changes in the lives of the veterans and the care givers.

I had a meeting up in the director's office, and one of the ladies asked me why I took so long to come see them about this situation. I stated I was up here many times and got the run around, as she looked at the records that was tainted with the blog and the doctors' personal statement. She looked at me and then back to the records and said, "See, this is how people get fired." Me as a veteran by me reading some of Title 38 Federal Rules and Regulation and asking veteran service officers questions and going to these round tables at the VA with my wife has helped us understand that this system is pass broke; it needs to be revamped. I can say that the majority of the time the director's office did not know of these incidents until you bring it to their attention. I'll give them the benefit of the doubt, and the best way that I know is attending these round tables. Board of veterans appeals are there along with service officers from DAV, VFW, Purple Heart as well as the directors staff and chief medical doctors. Sometimes you have to hurry up and wait but continue to come and voice your concerns until the problem is solved. I'm not telling you something that I haven't done. I'm still doing and learn and passing this ammunition to the next veteran.

CHAPTER 13

Are VA Employees Robbing Taxpayers and Disabled Veterans?

Ignoring, Concealing, Altering, Rejecting, and Expelling

Late disclosures of a mystery VA representative site may generate another examination concerning charges that C&P inspectors might plan against privileges of veterans with PTSD.

Look at additional on an old law we took a gander at that may apply to VA representatives who degrade VA laws and strategy in quest for their own particular increases to the detriment of veterans.

Recently, we secured the surreptitious compensation and pension made or managed by two VA therapists. No less than one of those therapists straightforwardly states VA analysts ought to assess veterans with an antagonistic, protection evaluator objective rather than the genius petitioner, opportunity to be vindicated target that is the rule that everyone must follow.

Take that one case and consider the various cases the nation over where journalists archive occurrences where VA authorities abuse the law and privileges of veterans for their own pick up in think demonstrations of resistance of the law.

So today, we thought it may be valuable to discuss how this old law that concentrated on decision issues may offer ascent to some new thoughts with regards to the guiltiness of scheme against your rights by VA representatives. All it takes are at least two to share in destroying your life to have a potential infringement of the law.

At the point when this happens, are these government representatives unlawfully scheming against you? Are these demonstrations infringing upon the law? Both answers might be a boisterous, "Yes!"

Conspiracy against Rights Is Punishable by Law

These individuals may be guilty of "Conspiracy Against Rights" under Section 241 of Title 18. According to the department of justice, it is unlawful for two or more individuals to agree together to injury, threaten, or intimidate another person related to that person's free exercise or enjoyment of any rights or privileges secured by the law or the Constitution.

Are my disability benefits and health care rights guaranteed under the law and Constitution? Yes.

Does the law require that one party to the conspiracy overtly do anything prior to the conspiracy being a crime? No.

What is unique about this law is that it does not require an overt act prior to the conspiracy being a crime. Violations of this law, conspiracy against rights are punishable in prison of up to a life term or the death penalty, depending on the facts and injury, if any, related to the criminal conduct.

That most certainly is one stiff penalty for violating a person's rights through a conspiracy.

The Law

TITLE 18, U.S.C., SECTION 241

If two or more persons conspire to injure, oppress, threaten, or intimidate any person in any State, Territory, Commonwealth, Possession, or District in the free exercise or enjoyment of any right or privilege secured to him by the Constitution or laws of the United States, or because of his having so exercised the same...

They shall be fined under this title or imprisoned not more than ten years, or both; and if death results from the acts committed in violation of this section or if such acts include kidnapping or an attempt to kidnap, aggravated sexual abuse or an attempt to commit aggravated sexual abuse, or an attempt to kill, they shall be fined under this title or imprisoned for any term of years or for life, or both, or may be sentenced to death.

We know veterans have a vested property ideal in their handicap benefits once granted and resultant due process rights in light of our Constitution. We know VA likes to rethink veterans with PTSD like clockwork in the occasion the veteran enhances or regresses. These things are given.

Can harm come from an anti-veteran exam? What happens if two C&P analysts choose to work as one with VA clinicians and others on the mystery CP examiner to decrease veterans' benefits? Imagine a scenario in which their activities bring about conveying ill-disposed PTSD exams in a way in opposition to the law. Imagine a scenario in which that activity brings about a lower incapacity rating for various veterans or some other sort of mischief. We might talk more than negligible negligence here.

A few naysayers presumably think these clinicians are helping citizens out by filtering through malingerers. Malingering implies the individual is putting forth a false expression with learning of the misrepresentation to pick up favorable position—essentially conferring extortion. In any case, the lead these men advocate for is unlawful as well as possibly hurtful. It accepts the individual is lying and requires an analyst to take part in antagonistic addressing. Antagonistic addressing could candidly hurt a veteran with PTSD. It could likewise monetarily hurt a veteran where the antagonistic nature brings about the veteran surrendering their advantages to keep away from the damage of ill-disposed scrutinizing at regular intervals for the PTSD reconsideration.

These strategies were to a great extent created by insurance agencies to spare cash on the backs of disabled individuals. However, are the strategies legitimized? They're legitimized as long as congress allows the VA to get away with this nonsense by not telling the true. The higher staff should also be held accountable at the VA hospital as well as the regional office. The doctors need to be specialized in the field of PTSD and not, for instance, podiatry. Taxpayers get robbed as well as the disabled veterans who fight and are still fighting for *freedom* and also die, waiting for the VA to do right.

I—gnoring
C—oncealing
A—ltering
R—ejecting
E—xpelling

Veterans Affairs:
Benefits for Service-Connected Disabilities

Summary

Congress provides various benefits to American veterans and their dependents through the United States Department of Veterans Affairs (VA). One of these benefits is *disability compensation*, which is a monthly cash benefit program for veterans currently impaired from past service-connected activities.

A claim for disability compensation is initially analyzed by the VA at the local level to determine: 1) whether the claimant is considered a "veteran" (eligible for benefits); 2) whether the veteran qualifies for disability compensation (entitled to benefits); 3) the extent of the impairment and the "rate" of the disability; and 4) the effective date for the compensation.

Three requirements to qualify for disability compensation are: 1) medical diagnosis of the current impairment; 2) evidence of an in-service occurrence or an aggravation of the disease or injury; and 3) medical proof of a connection between the in-service incident or aggravation of an injury or illness and the current disability. The requisite standard of proof and certain medical presumptions are set by statute. The VA is required to provide assistance to the veteran in his/her case preparation by providing records and medical examinations. Special rules have been established for certain specific situations involving combat veterans, prisoners of war, and veterans exposed to Agent Orange.

If the veteran is found eligible for disability compensation, the VA then uses the Schedule for Rating Disabilities (SRD) to set the amount of earnings impairment on a percentage basis; the higher the percentage, the greater the compensation will be. Certain complications arise with the use of the rating system. A veteran's rating may be increased or decreased over time — depending on his/her medical condition. Rating decisions may be appealed administratively.

Legislation passed in the First Session of the 110th Congress increased the 2008 monthly disability compensation payments. Other legislation has been introduced that would provide veterans a cost-of-living (COLA) for their VA benefits equal to the COLA for Social Security benefits. The 110th Congress has considered additional legislation that may affect service-connected disabilities. One bill would change the manner in which disabled veterans could qualify to receive Social Security Disability Insurance (SSDI) benefits. Several bills have been introduced to deal with the claims processing backlog at the VA and issues related to the receipt of disability benefits.

Contents

Introduction 1
    Veterans' Disability Programs 1
    The "Local Determination" 1
    Requirements for Disability Compensation 2
    Medical Proof of a Connection Between the In-Service Incident or
        Aggravation of an Injury/Illness and the Current Disability 4

The VA's Obligations in the Preparation/Presentation of
    the Veteran's Case and Certain Presumptions 5
    Standard of Proof 5
    Assistance in Case Preparation 5
    Certain Presumptions 6
        Presumption of Medical Soundness 6
        Special Rules for Certain In-Service Occurrences 6

The VA Rating System 7
    Schedule for Rating Disabilities (SRD) 7
    Application of the Rating System 8
        Complications in the Use of the Rating System 8
        Changes in Veterans' Ratings 9
        Special Monthly Compensation (SMC) 9
        Zero Percent Evaluation 9
        Periodic Examinations 9
        Appeals from Ratings 9
    Evaluation of the Rating System 10

Current Legislation 10
    Veterans' COLA (Cost-of-Living Adjustment) 10
    Social Security Disability Insurance (SSDI) Benefits 11
    Veterans' Claims Backlog and Related Issues 11

Veterans Affairs:
Benefits for Service-Connected Disabilities

Introduction

Veterans' Disability Programs

Congress, through the United States Department of Veterans Affairs (VA), provides a wide variety of services and benefits to veterans and to certain members of their families.[1]

Two disability programs are administered by the VA. These programs pay monthly cash benefits to certain disabled veterans.[2] *Disability compensation*, the focus of this report, provides a monthly cash benefit if the veteran is at least 10% disabled[3] as a consequence of his/her military service — which is considered to be a *service-connected disability*. A veteran applying for service-connected disability compensation does not need to be totally disabled, have low income, or wartime military service. In contrast, a *disability pension* may be paid to a *wartime*[4] veteran with limited income, who is no longer able to work, or is at least age 65. A disability pension is not related to a service-connected injury or medical condition and takes into account the material needs of the veteran; it is a "needs-based" pension.[5]

The "Local Determination"

The VA analyzes each veteran's claim for disability compensation at the VA regional office closest to the veteran's residence, called the "local determination." This determination involves a four-step adjudication process of the veteran's claim.

---

[1] See generally *Federal Benefits for Veterans and Dependents*, published by the Departments of Veterans Affairs (2008 edition). (Hereinafter cited as "*Federal Benefits*.") See [http://www1.va.gov/opa/vadocs/fedben.pdf] for the publication online. See CRS Report RL33113, *Veterans Affairs: Basic Eligibility for Disability Benefit Programs*, by Douglas Reid Weimer (cited to afterward as "RL33113"). This report deals with the fundamental requirements for disability benefit programs.

[2] *Id.*

[3] The severity of the veteran's disability is evaluated by the VA and a determination is made as to what percentage of employment capacity is impaired. See discussion below.

[4] See CRS Report RL33113.

[5] For further discussion of a disability pension or a non-service-connected pension, see CRS Report RL33113.

First, the VA determines the claimant's basic eligibility to receive VA benefits. A determination is made as to whether the claimant was discharged or separated under other than dishonorable conditions,[6] whether the claimant had "active service,"[7] and whether the claimant's condition is based upon the veteran's willful misconduct.[8]

Second, if the claimant is found eligible for benefits,[9] the VA then determines whether the veteran qualifies for in-service disability compensation.

Third, if the VA determines that the veteran is entitled to disability compensation, the VA then evaluates the extent of the disability and makes a determination of the percentage of the disability based upon the "Schedule for Rating Disabilities,"[10] which is sometimes referred to as the "SRD" and/or the "VASRD." Findings adverse to the interests of the veteran may be appealed administratively.

Fourth, the VA establishes the effective date for the award.

Requirements for Disability Compensation[11]

The purpose of disability compensation is to assist currently disabled veterans whose injury is connected to military service, and to that end, a veteran[12] must meet three basic criteria to the VA's satisfaction.

- *One:* A recent medical diagnosis of a *current* impairment, disability, or disease.

- *Two:* Medical or, on occasion, lay evidence of an *in-service* occurrence or aggravation of the disease or injury.

- *Three:* Medical proof of a *connection* between the in-service occurrence or aggravation of an injury or illness and the current disability.

Each of these requirements is examined below.

---

[6] See CRS Report RL33113.

[7] *Id.* at 4-5.

[8] *Id.* at 7-8.

[9] Hence, the claimant becomes a "veteran" for purposes of benefits.

[10] 38 U.S.C. § 1155; 38 C.F.R. § 4. See discussion below.

[11] See Barton F. Stichman et al., *Veterans Benefits Manual* at § 3.1.5. (Hereinafter cited as "*Veterans Benefits Manual.*")

[12] For the purposes of this report, it is assumed that the claimant/applicant has met the very basic eligibility requirements for VA benefits. The claimant/applicant will be referred to as the "veteran" for the remainder of this report.

CRS-3

Medical Evidence of the Current Impairment or Disability

Disability compensation is available only to veterans with current disabilities.[13] Although a veteran may have had an illness or injury during his/her service time, the mere fact that this occurred is not compensable.

To provide evidence of the current medical problem, the veteran may submit medical records of the current diagnosis and/or treatment. Letters from physicians may be added to the record. Generally speaking, lay evidence of a medical condition is not sufficient. The VA has certain duties to assist veterans in the application process.[14] The VA must assist by providing the veteran with the appropriate records.[15] Usually, the VA is required to provide veterans with a medical exam in order to diagnose a current medical condition.[16] However, certain circumstances may exist under which the VA may not be required to provide such an examination or assistance to the veteran.[17] In addition, the VA must advise veterans of incomplete applications[18] and evidence which is needed to evaluate the veteran's claim.[19]

Evidence of an In-Service Occurrence or Aggravation of the Disease or Injury

The veteran's second requirement for disability compensation is that there is medical or, under certain circumstances, lay evidence of an in-service occurrence or aggravation of a disease or injury. The in-service requirement is construed broadly. A disability incident or onset of disability is not required to be related to the veteran's military responsibilities and is covered even if it occurred during leave.[20] Further, the evidence submitted on the record must only demonstrate that it is as likely as not that there was an in-service aggravation or occurrence of a disease or injury. When there is nearly equal positive and negative evidence regarding a material issue, the Secretary is required to give the benefit of the doubt to the veteran.[21]

---

[13] 38 U.S.C. §§ 1110, 1131. These provisions deal with the basic entitlement for disability compensation.

[14] 38 U.S.C. § 5103A.

[15] 38 U.S.C. §§ 5103A(b),(c).

[16] 38 U.S.C. § 5103A(d).

[17] 38 U.S.C. § 5103A(a)(2).

[18] 38 U.S.C. § 5102(b).

[19] 38 U.S.C. § 5103(a).

[20] For example, a veteran may receive compensation for a medical condition that resulted from a sports injury incurred during in-service time. See *Veterans Benefit Manual* at §3.1.1.1.

[21] 38 U.S.C. § 5107(b).

CRS-4

The veteran must submit corroborating evidence of the incident.[22] He/she must prepare and submit a statement describing the occurrence, disease, or injury in detail, along with the circumstances surrounding the event. The type of evidence that the veteran must submit may depend upon the type of injury or disease which is being connected to the time of service. For example, a veteran who sustained a fall while in-service might produce evidence of medical treatment for the fall at the time of its occurrence and evidence from military personnel who witnessed the fall.

Medical Proof of a Connection Between the In-Service Incident or Aggravation of an Injury/Illness and the Current Disability

This third element requires that there must be a *link* between the current injury or illness (requirement 1) and that the disease, injury, or event happened during a period of military service (requirement 2). This requirement is sometimes known as service-connected, the "service connection," or the nexus requirement.

Statutes and regulations require proof of one of five types of connections. *One:* there is a direct connection between the current disability and an incident that happened during the period of military service.[23] *Two:* the current medical condition existed prior to service but was exacerbated during service.[24] *Three:* the current medical problem did not appear during military service, but is presumed to have begun or be connected with something that occurred during service, either by statute or by VA regulation.[25] *Four:* the present problem is the result of a primary medical condition, and that condition is connected to a period of military service.[26] *Five:* the condition is the result of an injury caused by VA health service, VA

Need to do this

---

[22] 38 C.F.R. § 3.303.

[23] 38 C.F.R. §§ 3.303(a), 3.304, 3.305. See also 38 U.S.C. § 1154. In determining whether the current condition relates to the in-service problem, the VA determines whether the problem is *acute* or *chronic*. An acute problem is considered to be a problem of relatively short duration. A chronic condition is of lengthy duration and may return.

[24] 38 U.S.C. § 1153; 38 C.F.R. § 3.306(a). If the disability existed prior to service, the VA must ascertain whether there was an *increase in the disability during service*. The preexisting problem will not be considered to be aggravated by service if the VA determines that the exacerbation resulted from the natural progression of the disease.

[25] 38 U.S.C. §§ 1112, 1116, 1133; 38 C.F.R. §§ 3.307-3.309; 38 C.F.R. § 3.313(b). If the disability claimed is a disease which was not diagnosed or recorded on the veteran's service record, the VA is required to ascertain whether *incubation time* for the disease could have started during in-service time (38 C.F.R. § 3.03(d)).

[26] 38 C.F.R. § 3.310(a). If the disability claimed cannot be determined to be in-service, either directly or by exacerbation, the VA will then decide whether the problem may be *service-connected on a secondary basis*. This reasoning is based on the theory that it was proximately caused by a service-connected condition. For instance, a primary disease is contracted in-service. A related, secondary disease develops as a result of the primary disease.

training/rehabilitation services, or by participation in a VA sponsored work therapy program.[27]

In order to establish this connection, it is necessary to have adequate medical evidence in the claim.[28] What this signifies is that for the in-service connection to be approved, the veteran is required to have medical proof that the disease, injury, or event which occurred during service *actually caused* the veteran's current disability.

The VA's Obligations in
the Preparation/Presentation of
the Veteran's Case and Certain Presumptions

The VA is required by law to use certain standards in the review of a veteran's claims, and the VA has certain statutory obligations in the preparation of the veteran's case. In addition, statute and regulations provide for certain presumptions of disability as a result of certain occurrences. These standards, requirements, and presumptions are summarized below.

Standard of Proof

As explained, to receive disability benefits evidence is required to prove a connection between an in-service incident and a current disability, but in assessing evidence on these elements the veteran is to be given the "benefit of the doubt."[29] The statute provides that "When there is an approximate balance of positive and negative evidence regarding any issue material to the determination of a matter, the Secretary shall give the benefit of the doubt to the claimant."[30] Regulations provide that when reasonable doubt arises, such doubt will be resolved in favor of the claimant.[31] Hence, in order to satisfy this element, the submitted medical evidence generally needs to show that it is as likely as not that there is a connection between the in-service injury, occurrence, or illness and the current disability.

Assistance in Case Preparation

The VA has a responsibility to assist the veteran in developing a claim. Among other things, the VA is required to advise the veteran of the type of evidence that will need to be submitted to substantiate the claim.[32]

---

[27] 38 U.S.C. § 1151.

[28] 38 U.S.C. § 5107.

[29] 38 U.S.C. § 5107(b).

[30] *Id.*

[31] 38 C.F.R. § 3.102.

[32] 38 U.S.C. § 5103(a).

The VA also must make service and medical records available to veterans for the preparation of their cases.[33] Such records are often crucial in proving the veteran's claim. In many instances, the VA is required to provide veterans with a *medical examination* in order to diagnose the current medical condition.[34] However, under certain circumstances the VA may not be required to provide assistance to the veteran.[35]

Certain Presumptions

In its analysis of certain claims, the VA is required by statute and/or regulation to make certain presumptions.

Presumption of Medical Soundness. In evaluating a veteran's claim, the VA generally presumes that the veteran entered the service in sound medical condition.[36] This may assist the veteran in proving a claim by making it difficult for the VA to claim that the condition or disease existed prior to service. However, if the medical impairment was noted at the time of entry into service, the veteran may have to prove that the condition was exacerbated in-service. If the VA is able to prove by "clear and unmistakable evidence" that the disease or injury was in existence prior to service, and that it was not worsened during service, the veteran's claim will be denied.

Special Rules for Certain In-Service Occurrences. Special rules exist under which the VA is required to consider a service-connected problem by presumption. For example, certain diseases associated with exposure to Agent Orange will be presumed to be service-related in the case of Vietnam veterans. [37]

➤ A similar regulation holds that veterans who were held prisoners of war, or who served in combat, can be presumed to have suffered traumatic, stressful events during their military service.[38] Similarly, combat veterans have special rules applicable to them in proving an in-service injury, or other incident.[39] Usually, if a combat veteran states that he/she suffered a disease, injury, or other event during combat, the VA will usually accept that statement as fact. This is the case even if there are no service records to substantiate the claim.

---

[33] 38 U.S.C. §§ 5103A(b), (c).

[34] 38 U.S.C. § 5103A(d).

[35] 38 U.S.C. § 5103A(a)(2).

[36] 38 U.S.C. § 1111.

[37] 38 C.F.R. § 3.307(a)(6)(iii).

[38] 38 C.F.R. § 3.304(f).

[39] 38 U.S.C. § 1154(b); 38 C.F.R. § 3.304(d),(f).

The VA Rating System

Congress has established by statute a rating system to categorize a veteran's degree of disability for in-service injuries.[40] This system is implemented by the VA through a series of complex regulations and procedures.

After the VA determines that a disability is service-connected, the VA regional office goes through a review process (the "rating activity") to determine the disability rating (on a percentage basis). As used by the VA, the term "disability" is defined as "the average impairment in earning capacity" that results from diseases, injuries, or their resultant aftermath.[41]

Schedule for Rating Disabilities (SRD)

By authority of Congress the VA set up the Schedule for Rating Disabilities ("SRD"), which rates various disabilities on a percentage basis.[42] The statute provides for ten grades of disability,[43] and the higher the disability determination, the higher is the monthly compensation that the veteran receives. The VA determines the disability level for an eligible veteran, and Congress sets the compensation rates for veterans based on ratings.[44]

Again, in making individual determinations, the VA and the Board of Veterans' Appeals (BVA) apply the various ratings of the SRD.[45] The SRD is detailed: various sections deal with injuries or diseases that impact particular body functions/parts, including the musculoskeletal system,[46] eyes,[47] and other functions such as hearing, infectious diseases, respiratory system, cardiovascular system, digestive system, genitourinary system, gynecological conditions, and other functions. Each of these sections of the SRD (dealing with a particular body part or function) has a series of medical diagnoses with a numerical diagnostic code (dc) that breaks down

---

[40] 38 U.S.C. § 1155.

[41] 38 C.F.R. § 4.1.

[42] 38 U.S.C. § 1155.

[43] 10% through 100%.

[44] The current monthly rates, effective on December 1, 2007, are as follows: an unmarried veteran without dependents and with a 10% disability receives $117 per month. The rates increase to a 100% disability payment of $2,527 per month (for an unmarried veteran without dependents). For rate tables and a compensation calculator, see [http://www.vba.va.gov/bln/21/rates/comp01.htm]. *The payment rates are not automatically adjusted for inflation, and are only increased if Congress passes enabling legislation.* Congress usually grants an increase based on the consumer price index or the cost-of-living formula used to determine the Social Security old age increase. The 2008 rates were set by P.L. 110-111, 110th Cong., 1st Sess. (November 5, 2007), the Veterans' Compensation Cost-of-Living Adjustment Act of 2007.

[45] 38 C.F.R. § 4.1.

[46] 38 C.F.R. §§ 4.40 to 4.73.

[47] 38 C.F.R. §§ 4.75 to 4.84a.

percentages of disability[48] based upon the severity of the disability. Each degree of disability under each dc has a description of the symptoms that the claimant veteran must have in order to qualify for that rating. The disability degree increases with the increase in the severity of the symptoms.

Application of the Rating System[49]

Applying this rating system, the VA examines the veteran's medical records to determine the medical diagnosis for the veteran's service-connected disability. The VA then finds the applicable diagnostic code for the disability and finds the degree of disability that is appropriate to the symptoms and diagnosis of the veteran's condition. If a rating falls between two ratings, and the symptoms are closer to the higher rating, then the higher rating will be selected.[50] In makings its determination, the VA examines all of the available evidence, including service records, lay statements, and medical records and other evidence.[51]

Complications in the Use of the Rating System. When the VA applies the diagnostic code(s) to veterans' claims, a number of variables come into play, some of which may be quite complex. And while every rating has unique circumstances, VA ratings in similar cases may not always seem consistent. Having to make fine distinctions within an intricate rating system based on a reading of a veteran's symptoms inevitably leads to some claims that a rating is "wrong" or "underrated."

Another complication in the rating process is that a medical condition may be able to be rated under more than one diagnostic code, sometimes to the detriment of the veteran. In addition, not all disabilities and their symptoms and complications are listed on the rating chart, in which case an analogous condition may be used for the rating.[52]

A further complication in the rating system occurs when a veteran has two or more service-connected disabilities. In such a circumstance, the overall percentage of disability is determined by combining the individual ratings, but *not by adding them up together*. To calculate the appropriate combined rating, the VA makes a determination by considering each impairment in the order of its severity. Direction

---

[48] See 38 C.F.R. § 4.84a for an example of the ratings and diagnostic codes chart for impairment of vision.

[49] See CRS Report RL33991, *Disability Evaluation of Military Servicemembers*, by Christine Scott, Sidath Viranga Panangala, Sarah A. Lister, and Charles A. Henning.

[50] 38 C.F.R. § 4.7.

[51] 38 C.F.R. § 3.103(d).

[52] 38 C.F.R. § 4.20. However, if a case when a veteran's disability is so extraordinary or unusual that an analogy cannot be made through use of the rating charts, an "extraschedular rating" for a veteran may be made (38 C.F.R. § 3.321(b)).

on how to make these determinations is contained in the "Combined Rating Table" in the VA regulations.[53]

Changes in Veterans' Ratings. Should the severity of the service-connected disability increase over time, the veteran may apply for an increase in the rated percentage of disability.[54] Similarly, should the condition improve, the ratings percentage may be decreased, and the monthly payments would decrease.

Special Monthly Compensation (SMC). If a veteran has severe disabilities,[55] he/she may be entitled to special monthly compensation (SMC) which provides compensation payments at a rate higher than the 100% rate.[56] In addition to the SMC, certain veterans with severe disabilities that require daily assistance or regular health services may be eligible for extra compensation.[57]

Zero Percent Evaluation. If the degree of disability from a service-connected incident does not impair earning capacity, a veteran may receive a 0% rating.[58] However, even a noncompensable evaluation under certain circumstances may entitle the veteran to preferences in federal or state employment and VA health care. A noncompensable evaluation may also be used to document a medical condition if it subsequently worsens.

Periodic Examinations. Following the award of compensation benefits, the VA may require periodic examinations to determine whether the condition is constant in its severity and that continued payment of disability compensation is warranted.[59] The VA is authorized to reexamine veterans receiving compensation benefits at any time. However, under certain circumstances — if the condition is static — the VA may not schedule review examinations.

Appeals from Ratings. Some veterans may not be satisfied with their disability rating, and may wish to appeal. Such an appeal is first undertaken at the local VA level and may eventually proceed to the Court of Veterans Claims ("Court").[60] The Court examines whether the VA considered all of the appropriate facts and set forth a satisfactory explanation for its choice and application of the diagnostic code.

---

[53] 38 U.S.C. § 1157; 38 C.F.R. § 4.25.

[54] See "Compensation and Pension Benefits Page" at VA website; *A Summary of VA Benefits: Putting Veterans First*, VA Pamphlet 21-00-1 (January 2006); see also [http://www.va.gov] (click on "Benefits," and then go to "Compensation and Pension Benefits Page").

[55] Such disabilities may involve anatomical loss or the loss of use of a hand or foot.

[56] 38 U.S.C. § 1114(k); 38 C.F.R. § 3.350.

[57] 38 U.S.C. § 1114(r)(2); 38 C.F.R. § 3.352.

[58] Many conditions listed within the ratings tables are rated as 0. See also 38 C.F.R. § 4.31.

[59] 38 C.F.R. § 3.327(a).

[60] See CRS Report RS22561, *Veterans Affairs: The U.S. Court of Appeals for Veterans Claims — Judicial Review of VA Decision Making*, by Douglas Reid Weimer.

[handwritten: Special M C for loss of cervix related to 1989 Rape.]

Evaluation of the Rating System

A 2005 Government Accountability Office (GAO) study, *Veterans' Disability Benefits — Claims Processing Challenges and Opportunities for Improvements*[61] evaluated certain aspects of the disability compensation process. GAO noted that the VA provided $30 billion in cash disability benefits to more than 3.4 million veterans and their survivors in FY2004.[62] GAO found that the VA has continuing challenges in the disability compensation process, including large numbers of pending claims and long processing times.[63]

Another issue that GAO highlighted is the lack of consistency and accuracy of rating decisions at and among the VA's 57 regional offices.[64] Consequently, veterans with similar disabilities may receive different evaluations, and hence may receive significantly different compensation from the different VA regional offices. GAO also noted that the VA's evaluative process has not kept pace with recent developments in medical technology.[65]

GAO uncovered another issue — that more recent veterans with severe injuries would appear to favor a lump sum compensation payment, as opposed to monthly compensation payments over an extended period of time.[66]

Current Legislation[67]

Veterans' COLA (Cost-of-Living Adjustment)

Congress typically has passed legislation annually to provide a COLA in veterans disability compensation equal to the COLA automatically provided under permanent law to recipients of Social Security disability. However, this COLA is not automatic, and must be enacted annually. The Veterans' Compensation Cost-of-Living Adjustment Act of 2007[68] increased, effective December 1, 2007, the rates (dollar amounts) of veteran's disability compensation (as well as for additional compensation for dependents, the clothing allowance for certain disabled veterans,

---

[61] GAO-06-283T, Testimony before the Committee on Veterans' Affairs, House of Representatives; Statement for the Record by Cynthia A. Bascetta, Director, Education, Workforce, and Income Security Issues (GAO) (December 7, 2005).

[62] *Id.* at 1.

[63] *Id.* at 2, 4-6.

[64] *Id.* at 5-7.

[65] *Id.* at 8-9.

[66] *Id.* at 9-10.

[67] See CRS Report RL33985, *Veterans Benefits Issues in the 110th Congress*, by Carol D. Davis, Coordinator, Shannon S. Loane, Meredith Peterson, Christine Scott, Libby Perl, and Douglas Reid Weimer.

[68] P.L. 110-111, 110th Cong., 1st Sess (November 5, 2007).

and the dependency and indemnity compensation for surviving spouses and children).[69]

S. 161 (sponsored by Senator John Thune),[70] **H.R. 402** (sponsored by Representative Joe Knollenberg),[71] and **S. 1315** (sponsored by Senator Daniel K. Akaka)[72] would create an automatic veterans' COLA based on the Social Security adjustment.

Social Security Disability Insurance (SSDI) Benefits

H.R. 2943 (introduced by Representative John P. Sarbannes)[73] would change the manner in which disabled veterans could qualify to receive SSDI benefits. If enacted, the bill would permit veterans with service-connected disabilities that are rated and certified by the VA as total, to be eligible for SSDI benefits without having to be evaluated by the Social Security Administration (SSA) if they meet the other requirements for SSDI benefits. At the present time, SSA evaluates all applicants (veterans and non-veterans) to determine their eligibility for SSDI benefits.[74]

Veterans' Claims Backlog and Related Issues

Presently, there is a large number of pending veterans' claims before the VA. According to the VA, which tracks these figures, for the week ended May 3, 2008, there were 396,898 rating cases pending.[75] This compares to a backlog of 405,248 rating cases from the same time period in 2007.[76] Concern over this backlog has been expressed by legislators and veterans' groups.

In response to this backlog, several bills have been introduced in the 110th Congress that would impact disability determinations by the VA. The proposed Wounded Warrior Assistance Act of 2007 is pending in the House, **H.R. 1538**

---

[69] This law amended 38 U.S.C. § 1114 and established increased monthly payments.

[70] S. 161, 110th Cong., 1st Sess (2007). The bill was introduced and was referred to the Senate Committee on Veterans' Affairs on January 4, 2007.

[71] H.R. 402, 110th Cong., 1st Sess (2007). The bill was introduced on January 11, 2007, and was referred to the House Subcommittee on Disability Assistance and Memorial Affairs on March 2, 2007.

[72] S. 1315, 110th Cong., 1st Sess (2007). The bill was introduced on May 7, 2007, and passed the Senate and was received in the House on April 24, 2008.

[73] H.R. 2943, 110th Cong., 1st Sess (2007). The bill was introduced and was referred to the House Committee on Ways and Means on June 28, 2007.

[74] See CRS Report RL32279, *Primer on Disability Benefits: Social Security Disability Insurance (SSDI) and Supplemental Security Income (SSI)*, by Scott Szymendera.

[75] The VA breaks these figures down in very detailed "workload reports." For more information, go to the VA website, [http://www.va.gov], and search under "workload reports." Then go to "Monday Morning Workload Report" and access for the current statistics.

[76] *Id.*

(introduced by Representative Ike Skelton),[77] and in the Senate, **S. 1283** (introduced by Senator Mark Pryor).[78] Both bills address disability evaluations, a study by the DOD and VA concerning their evaluation systems, and the possibility of combining the two systems.

H.R. 653 (sponsored by Representative Thomas M. Reynolds)[79] would have the Secretary of Veterans Affairs accept that an injury or disease is service-connected (if there is no clear and convincing proof to the contrary), based upon the sworn affidavit of a veteran who served in combat on or before July 27, 1953 (prior to or during the Korean War).

H.R. 797 (sponsored by Representative Tammy Baldwin), which was enacted into law,[80] expands disability compensation for veterans who are visually impaired in both eyes by using a standard definition of blindness used by other federal agencies.

H.R. 1435 (sponsored by Representative Joe Baca)[81] would direct the VA to conduct a pilot program with County Veterans Services Officers (CVSOs) in certain states. Certain claims requiring further development would be referred to the CVSOs. The CVSOs would be required to act as claimant advocates in developing such claims and have access to client information contained in the VA's Benefits Delivery Network.

H.R. 1444 (sponsored by Representative John Hall),[82] although not specifically addressing the backlog, would provide some benefits for those veterans awaiting their rating/appeal. The bill would require the Secretary of the VA to pay an interim benefit of $500 per month when a claim for veterans' benefits is remanded (referred back) by either the U.S. Court of Appeals for Veterans Claims or the Board of Veterans' Appeals, and the Secretary does not make a decision on the matter within 180 days of the date of the remand.

---

[77] H.R. 1538, 110th Cong., 1st Sess (2007). The bill was introduced on March 15, 2007, passed the House on March 28, 2007, and passed the Senate with an amendment by Unanimous Consent on July 25, 2007. The Senate ordered the measure printed as passed on September 5, 2007.

[78] S. 1283, 110th Cong., 1st Sess (2007). The bill was introduced and was referred to the Senate Committee on Armed Services on May 3, 2007.

[79] H.R. 654, 110th Cong., 1st Sess (2007). The bill was introduced on January 24, 2007, and was referred to the House Subcommittee on Disability Assistance and Memorial Affairs on March 2, 2007.

[80] P.L. 110-157, 110th Cong., 1st Sess (December 12, 2007).

[81] H.R. 1435, 110th Cong., 1st Sess (2007). The bill was introduced on March 9, 2007, and the House Subcommittee on Disability Assistance and Memorial Affairs held hearings on April 17, 2007.

[82] H.R. 1444, 110th Cong., 1st Sess (2007). The bill was introduced on March 9, 2007, and the House Subcommittee on Disability Assistance and Memorial Affairs held hearings on April 17, 2007.

H.R. 1490 (sponsored by Representative Joe Donnelly)[83] would create a presumption of service-connectedness in claims for service-connected benefits unless the Secretary of the VA determines that there is positive evidence to the contrary. The bill would require the claimant to support the claim with proof of service in a conflict referred to in the claim, as well as a brief description of the nature, including the service connection, of the disability or claim. The Secretary would be required to redeploy, for the purpose of assisting veterans applying for benefits, those employees who are no longer needed to evaluate claims due to this presumption.

H.R. 1538 (sponsored by Representative Ike Skelton)[84] deals primarily with improving the management of medical care, personnel actions, and quality of life issues for members of the Armed Forces. The bill addresses disability evaluations, a study by DOD and the VA concerning their individual evaluation systems, and the possibility of combining the two systems. The bill would also streamline record keeping and the transfer of records from DOD to the VA. Some of the bill's provisions are similar to those of S. 1283, discussed below.

H.R. 2257 (sponsored by Representative Peter Welch)[85] would require the Secretary of the VA to increase the number of benefits claims representatives. The bill would require that no fewer than two claims representatives be located at each "vet center"[86] to provide readjustment counseling and related mental health services.

H.R. 2855 (sponsored by Representative Ciro Rodriguez)[87] would establish a Wounded Heroes Independent Review Board ("Board") to review certain cases involving a member of the Armed Forces or a veteran who was severely injured on or after September 11, 2001, while on active duty. Upon the request of a "Wounded Hero," the Board would expeditiously review the decision or determination of the VA or other federal department or agency relating to the eligibility for or scope of benefits, including health care or vocational rehabilitation benefits. Following a review, the Board would render a written advisory opinion relating to such eligibility or provision of such care or benefits. The advisory opinion would be "considered as

---

[83] H.R. 1490, 110th Cong., 1st Sess (2007). The bill was introduced on March 13, 2007, and the Subcommittee on Disability Assistance and Memorial Affairs held hearings on April 17, 2007.

[84] H.R. 1538, 110th Cong., 1st Sess (2007). The bill was introduced on March 15, 2007, passed the House on March 28, 2007, and passed the Senate with an amendment by Unanimous Consent on July 25, 2007. A message on Senate action was sent to the House on July 26, 2007. On September 5, 2007, the Senate ordered the measure to be printed as passed.

[85] H.R. 2257, 110th Cong., 1st Sess (2007). The bill was introduced on May 9, 2007, and was referred to the House Subcommittee on Disability Assistance and Memorial Affairs on May 11, 2007.

[86] These "centers" provide readjustment counseling and related mental health services to veterans (38 U.S.C. § 1712A(i)(1)).

[87] H.R. 2855, 110th Cong., 1st Sess (2007). The bill was introduced on June 25, 2007, and was referred to the House Subcommittee on Military Personnel on July 25, 2007.

CRS-14

evidence" by the BVA and the CAVC in any case with respect to the "Wounded Hero." An advisory opinion rendered by the Board would not be reviewed by any other official or by any court, whether by an action in the nature of mandamus or otherwise.

H.R. 3047 (sponsored by Representative Doug Lamborn)[88] would direct the Secretary of the VA to establish a work credit system for evaluating regional offices of the Veterans Benefits Administration (VBA) regarding veterans' claims processing. The Secretary would be required to develop and maintain an electronic claims processing system for processing veterans' disability compensation claims that utilizes medical and military service date to generate disability rating recommendations. The Secretary would also be required to maintain a regional office at which all such claims are exclusively processed electronically. The bill would direct the Secretary to contract with a private entity to evaluate the training and assessment programs for VBA employees.

H.R. 4084 (sponsored by Representative John Hall)[89] would direct the Secretary of the VA to contract with the Institute of Medicine, or other appropriate entity, to conduct a study analyzing the extent to which the Department of Veterans Affairs schedule for rating disability accounts for or should be amended to account, measure, and compensate for loss of quality of life to veterans due to a disability resulting from a personal injury suffered, or disease contracted, in the line of duty. The bill would also provide that if a veteran who is a claimant dies before completing the submission of a claim for benefits, the person who would receive any accrued benefits due to such veteran would be treated as the claimant for purposes of completing submission of the claim.

H.R. 5089 (sponsored by Representative John Barrow)[90] would propose to reform the veterans' disability determination process by requiring the Secretary of Veterans Affairs to pay disability compensation to certain veterans based on the concurring diagnosis of two physicians.

H.R. 5576 (sponsored by Representative Steve Buyer)[91] would make various improvements to the claims processing system of the VA. Among these improvements would be training for agents/attorneys representing veterans, quality control assessment for regional offices of the Veterans Benefits Administration (VBA), the electronic processing of claims, treatment of beneficiaries in the event of

---

[88] H.R. 3047, 110th Cong., 1st Sess (2007). The bill was introduced on July 16, 2007, and the House Subcommittee on Disability Assistance and Memorial Affairs held hearings on November 8, 2007.

[89] H.R. 4084, 110th Cong., 1st Sess (2007). The bill was introduced on November 6, 2007, and the House Subcommittee on Disability Assistance and Memorial Affairs held hearings on November 8, 2007.

[90] H.R. 5089, 110th Cong., 2nd Sess (2008). The bill was introduced and was referred to the House Committee on Veterans' Affairs on January 22, 2008.

[91] H.R. 5576, 110th Cong., 2nd Sess (2008). The bill was introduced on March 11, 2008, and was referred to the House Subcommittee on Disability Assistance and Memorial Affairs on March 14, 2008.

the death of the veteran before claim determination, evaluation of training and assessment programs for employees of the VBA, electronic monitoring of claim status, a pilot program permitting the submission of claims to any regional office of the VA, and other programs.

H.R. 5892 (sponsored by Representative John J. Hall)[92] would amend title 38 of the U.S. Code to direct the Secretary of the VA to modernize the disability benefits claims processing system of the VA to ensure the accurate and timely delivery of compensation to veterans and their families and survivors. Various disability benefit issues are covered in the bill.

S. 1283 (sponsored by Senator Mark Pryor)[93] deals primarily with improving the management of medical care, personnel actions, and quality of life issues for members of the Armed Forces. The bill addresses disability evaluations, a study by the DOD and the VA concerning their individual evaluation systems, and the possibility of combining the two systems. Some of the bill's provisions are similar to those of H.R. 1538, discussed above.

S. 1363 (sponsored by Senator Hillary Rodham Clinton),[94] the proposed Bridging the Gap for Wounded Warriors Act, would improve health care for severely injured members and former members of the armed forces. The bill would create a Department of Defense — Department of Veterans Affairs Office of Transition ("Office").[95] Among the functions of this Office would be to "develop uniform standards, to be applicable across the military departments and to the Department of Veterans Affairs, for the rating of disabilities incurred or aggravated by members of the Armed Forces during service in the Armed Forces."[96] The bill would also provide for the reform of the disability ratings system of the Department of Defense and the Department of Veterans Affairs.[97]

S. 2737 (sponsored by Senator Daniel K. Akaka),[98] the proposed Veterans' Ratings Schedule Review Act, would amend title 38 of the United States Code to grant jurisdiction to the U.S. Court of Appeals for Veterans Claims to review compliance of ratings for disabilities under the schedule of 38 U.S.C. § 1151 with the statutory requirements applicable to entitlement to disability compensation.

---

[92] H.R. 5892, 110th Cong., 2nd Sess (2008). The bill was introduced and was referred to the House Committee on Veterans' Affairs on April 24, 2008. On April 30, 2008, the Committee held a mark-up session and the bill was ordered to be reported.

[93] S. 1283, 110th Cong., 1st Sess (2007). The bill was introduced and was referred to the Senate Committee on Armed Services on May 3, 2007.

[94] S. 1363, 110th Cong., 1st Sess (2007). The bill was introduced and referred to the Senate Committee on Armed Services on May 10, 2007.

[95] S. 1363, § 3.

[96] Id. § 3(c)(5).

[97] Id. § 4.

[98] S. 2737, 110th Cong., 2nd Sess (2008). The bill was introduced and was referred to the Senate Committee on Veterans' Affairs on March 10, 2008.

http://www.benefits.va.gov/warms/bookc.asp#d

This is the table chart that the VA uses to determine your disability rating. The website above could also help you when doing your claim. *Please read!* Very important information.

Combined Ratings Table

Table 1, Combined Ratings Table, results from the consideration of the efficiency of the individual as affected first by the most disabling condition then by the less disabling condition then by other less disabling conditions, if any, in the order of severity. Thus, a person having a sixty percent disability is considered forty percent efficient. Proceeding from this forty percent efficiency, the effect of a further thirty percent disability is to leave only seventy percent of the efficiency remaining after consideration of the first disability or twenty-eight percent efficiency altogether. The individual is thus seventy-two percent disabled, as shown in table 1, opposite sixty percent and under thirty percent.

(a) To use table 1, the disabilities will first be arranged in the exact order of their severity, beginning with the greatest disability and then combined with use of table 1 as hereinafter indicated. For example, if there are two disabilities, the degree of one disability will be read in the left column and the degree of the other in the top row, whichever is appropriate. The figures appearing in the space where the column and row intersect will represent the combined value of the two. This combined value will then be converted to the nearest number divisible by ten, and combined values ending in five will be adjusted upward. Thus, with a fifty percent disability and a thirty percent disability, the combined value will be found to be sixty-five percent, but the sixty-five percent must be converted to seventy percent to represent the final degree of disability. Similarly, with a disability of forty percent and another disability of twenty percent, the combined value is found to be fifty-two percent, but the fifty-two percent must be converted to the nearest degree divisible by ten, which is fifty percent. If there are more than two disabilities, the disabilities will also be arranged in the exact order of their severity and the combined value for the first two will be found as previously described for two disabilities. The combined value, exactly as found in table 1, will be combined with the degree of the third disability (in order of severity). The combined value for the three disabilities will be found in the space where the column and row intersect, and if there are only three disabilities will be converted to the nearest degree divisible by ten, adjusting final fives upward. Thus if there are three disabilities ratable at sixty percent, forty percent, and twenty percent, respectively, the combined value for the first two will be found opposite sixty and under forty and is seventy-six percent. This seventy-six percent will be combined with twenty and the combined value for the three is eighty-one percent. This combined value will be converted to the nearest degree divisible by ten which is eighty percent. The same procedure will be employed when there are four or more disabilities. (See table 1).

(b) Except as otherwise provided in this schedule, the disabilities arising from a single disease entity, e.g., arthritis, multiple sclerosis, cerebrovascular accident, etc., are to be rated separately as are all other disabling conditions, if any. All disabilities are then to be combined as described in paragraph (a) of this section. The conversion to the nearest degree divisible by ten will be done only once per rating decision, will follow the combining of all disabilities, and will be the last procedure in determining the combined degree of disability. (Authority: 38 U.S.C. 1155)

This is how you read this scale to find out what you are rated at, if your high number is seventy percent and your low number is thirty percent, look for the number thirty to your left then take it all the way until you reach seventy percent and that number should say seventy-nine percent rounded off your rating is eighty percent.

Table I—Combined Ratings Table

[10 combined with 10 is 19]

	10	20	30	40	50	60	70	80	90
19	27	35	43	51	60	68	76	84	92
20	28	36	44	52	60	68	76	84	92
21	29	37	45	53	61	68	76	84	92
22	30	38	45	53	61	69	77	84	92
23	31	38	46	54	62	69	77	85	92
24	32	39	47	54	62	70	77	85	92
25	33	40	48	55	63	70	78	85	93
26	33	41	48	56	63	70	78	85	93
27	34	42	49	56	64	71	78	85	93
28	35	42	50	57	64	71	78	86	93
29	36	43	50	57	65	72	79	86	93
30	37	44	51	58	65	72	79	86	93
31	38	45	52	59	66	72	79	86	93
32	39	46	52	59	66	73	80	86	93
33	40	46	53	60	67	73	80	87	93
34	41	47	54	60	67	74	80	87	93
35	42	48	55	61	68	74	81	87	94
36	42	49	55	62	68	74	81	87	94
37	43	50	56	62	69	75	81	87	94
38	44	50	57	63	69	75	81	88	94
39	45	51	57	63	70	76	82	88	94
40	46	52	58	64	70	76	82	88	94
41	47	53	59	65	71	76	82	88	94
42	48	54	59	65	71	77	83	88	94
43	49	54	60	66	72	77	83	89	94
44	50	55	61	66	72	78	83	89	94

	10	20	30	40	50	60	70	80	90
45	51	56	62	67	73	78	84	89	95
46	51	57	62	68	73	78	84	89	95
47	52	58	63	68	74	79	84	89	95
48	53	58	64	69	74	79	84	90	95
49	54	59	64	69	75	80	85	90	95
50	55	60	65	70	75	80	85	90	95
51	56	61	66	71	76	80	85	90	95
52	57	62	66	71	76	81	86	90	95
53	58	62	67	72	77	81	86	91	95
54	59	63	68	72	77	82	86	91	95
55	60	64	69	73	78	82	87	91	96
56	60	65	69	74	78	82	87	91	96
57	61	66	70	74	79	83	87	91	96
58	62	66	71	75	79	83	87	92	96
59	63	67	71	75	80	84	88	92	96
60	64	68	72	76	80	84	88	92	96
61	65	69	73	77	81	84	88	92	96
62	66	70	73	77	81	85	89	92	96

Table I—Combined Ratings Table (cont.)

	10	20	30	40	50	60	70	80	90
63	67	70	74	78	82	85	89	93	96
64	68	71	75	78	82	86	89	93	96
65	69	72	76	79	83	86	90	93	97
66	69	73	76	80	83	86	90	93	97
67	70	74	77	80	84	87	90	93	97
68	71	74	78	81	84	87	90	94	97
69	72	75	78	81	85	88	91	94	97
70	73	76	79	82	85	88	91	94	97
71	74	77	80	83	86	88	91	94	97
72	75	78	80	83	86	89	92	94	97
73	76	78	81	84	87	89	92	95	97
74	77	79	82	84	87	90	92	95	97

75	78	80	83	85	88	90	93	95	98
76	78	81	83	86	88	90	93	95	98
77	79	82	84	86	89	91	93	95	98
78	80	82	85	87	89	91	93	96	98
79	81	83	85	87	90	92	94	96	98
80	82	84	86	88	90	92	94	96	98
81	83	85	87	89	91	92	94	96	98
82	84	86	87	89	91	93	95	96	98
83	85	86	88	90	92	93	95	97	98
84	86	87	89	90	92	94	95	97	98
85	87	88	90	91	93	94	96	97	99
86	87	89	90	92	93	94	96	97	99
87	88	90	91	92	94	95	96	97	99
88	89	90	92	93	94	95	96	98	99
89	90	91	92	93	95	96	97	98	99
90	91	92	93	94	95	96	97	98	99
91	92	93	94	95	96	96	97	98	99
92	93	94	94	95	96	97	98	98	99
93	94	94	95	96	97	97	98	99	99
94	95	95	96	96	97	98	98	99	99

(Authority: 38 U.S.C. 1155)

UNITED STATES DEPARTMENT OF VETERANS AFFAIRS:
THE THREE ADMINISTRATIONS

1. **Veteran Health Administration (VHA):** provides all forms of **healthcare** to veterans at VA hospitals, Community Based Outpatient Clinics (CBOCs), Community Living Centers (CLCs), Tele-Health, Home visits, and through Outreach. Also collaborates with the Office of Research and Development to promote ground breaking biomedical research.

2. **National Cemetery Administration**: provides burial and memorial benefits, and maintains the national cemeteries.

3. **Veterans Benefits Administration** (VBA): RESPONSIBLE FOR ALL VETERAN **BENEFIT PROGRAMS** including initial veteran registration, determines eligibility for benefits, and manages five benefits and entitlement programs: *1) Home Loan Guarantee; 2) Insurance; 3) Vocational Rehabilitation & Employment; 4) Education (GI Bill/Post 911/Montgomery); 5) Compensation & Pension Evaluation & Services; and 6) Retirement.*

*TIPS FOR MAKING A SUCCESSFUL TRANSITION *

- **Verify your enrollment status**, confirm demographic information, and provide copies of your updated DD214 form and final or new SC Disability Determination Ratings Evaluations to the Atlanta VAMC Registration and Enrollment Department.

- **Make sure to see your assigned PCT provider at least once a year so you will remain an established patient and active** on the provider's panel of patients. Make sure to do this even if you have a civilian provider. Please Note: Multiple " No Show" for scheduled appts could affect your SC Disability Rating ☺

- **Schedule a dental cleaning or exam within six months of your discharge date.** Call the Dental Clinic at 404-321-6111 ext. **3748** to schedule your appointment, even if it's post 6 months.

- **Register for the MyHealthEvet (MHV) Program and get upgraded to a PREMIUM LEVEL ACCOUNT.** This type of account will allow you to access your medical records from home, print your records at home, send your providers emails, and schedule refills of medications online. Go to the Veterans Learning Center or call **404-321-6111 ext. 4982** to schedule an appointment. Remote enrollment is available for those who are not able to enroll in person. The MHV Coordinator is Michael Burton and he can be contacted at (404)-235-3025. The website may be accessed at www.myhealth.va.gov .

- **Find out if you are eligible for VA Travel Benefits or VA Transportation Services.** You may be eligible for reimbursement of mileage to and from scheduled medical appointments. Call the Travel Reimbursement Office (404-3321-6111 ext. 6501 or ext. 5427) with any questions.

- **Ask questions, write down information, keep a calendar of appointments and write down names and numbers for all providers.** Keep copies of all your health records. Bring a friend or relative to appointments to provide support if you are able to do so.

- **Sign a release of information (ROI)** to allow your VA and civilian providers to work together to best manage your health care.

- **Ask questions as needed.** We are here to help you. Please call your TCM Care Manager for assistance. We are here to serve you and help you in any way we can. ☺

1

USEFUL CONTACT NUMBERS

Pertinent Phone Numbers and Information For Veterans

	Address	Phone Number	Website/Additional Information
VA/Telephone Resources			
Centralized Scheduling Office		404-321-6111 X1396	Call to schedule PC **new patient appointment** Veterans-this is the centralized scheduling number for them to use to make a new patient appointment with Primary Care. Please leave a message, and provider will call them back. ****Women Veterans:** Please indicate if you wish to be scheduled with the **Women's Wellness Primary Care**
Telephone Advice Program (TAP) Line		(404) 329-2222 Or 800-224-4087	Call to schedule future **Primary Care follow up visits** •CALL FOR PRESCRIPTION RENEWAL •GENERAL MEDICAL ADVICE •TO SCHEDULE, CANCEL OR RESCHEDULE APPOINTMENTS A NURSE WILL RESPOND TO YOUR TAP LINE CALL YOU MAY ALSO LEAVE A MESSAGE FOR YOUR PROVIDER
Medical Records	Atlanta VAMC	404-321-6111 Ext. 6040	
Empower Veterans Program	Atlanta VA CBOC		**Empower Veterans Program** coaches Veterans with chronic pain to live a fuller life by moving toward their own Wellness goals. -Initial evaluation from Program Doctor (typically occurs through E-Consult- PC Doctor to Program Doctor)
Veterans Choice Program		1-866-606-8198	**You are eligible if any of these situations apply to you:** • **You have been (or will be) waiting more than 30 days for VA medical care** • **You live more than 40 miles away from a VA**

| | | | medical care facility or face one of several <u>excessive travel burdens.</u>

To get started, you'll need to pick a health care provider, gather some information and give us a call in order to set up an appointment. We will work with you to ensure you are approved for care in your community and schedule you with a local care provider of your choice.
1. Step 1: Check if you are <u>eligible.</u>
2. Step 2: Explore which <u>doctors</u> are participating in your area.
3. Step 3: Make sure you have information on hand about any other health insurance coverage you may have.
4. Step 4: Call 1-866-606-819 to make sure you qualify and to schedule an appointment. When you call, we will:
• Ask for your ZIP code.
• Ask for your address.
• Check to make sure you are eligible for this program.
• Check which of your needs are covered by the VA.
• Ask for your preferred community provider. Unfortunately, not all providers will be eligible to participate so if your preferred provider is not available, we will recommend other providers in your area. |
| Nutrition and Food Services | Main Campus-Ground Floor | 404-321-6111 x 6820 | Veterans including inpatient and outpatient services. When appropriate, formula calculations, calorie counts or nutrient analyses, and basic nutrition |

			assessments can be completed via the computer system and any telephone within the system to facilitate timely treatments. *Requires consult from Doctor
Readjustment Counseling Services			
Lawrenceville Vet Center	930 River Centre Place Lawrenceville, GA 30043	(404) 728-4195	You may present as a walk in or call ahead to schedule an appointment
Atlanta Vet Center	1800 Phoenix Blvd., Bldg 400, Suite 404, College Park, GA 30349	(404) 321-6111, x5910	Individual counseling is available, as well as some support groups, family counseling services, etc. In an effort to better serve the veteran and family members, upon request Vet Centers will provide services after normal work hours and/or on weekends.
Marietta Vet Center	40 Dodd St., SE, Marietta, GA 30060	(404) 327-4954	
NAMI Family-to-Family Education Program	Atlanta VAMC Ground Floor, Mental Health Clinic, GB 151	(404) 321-6111, x6011	The NAMI Family-to-Family Education Program is a free 12-week course for family members (over 18 years of age) of Veterans living with mental illness; contact Dr. Erin Elliott for details if interested
Employment Resources			
The VA offers a number of resources for helping Veterans obtain and excel in employment both within and outside VA. Check out the resources below:		1-855-824-8387	**The Veteran Employment Services Office (VESO)** is a strategic program management office that provides employment and career management resources designed to attract, retain and support Veteran employees at VA and across the federal government, including those serving in the National Guard and Reserve. VESO develops and implements innovative and comprehensive programs, procedures and services to support federal Veteran recruitment and VA retention and reintegration. Programs and services include career services in VA, matching your experience to Federal job opportunities, recruitment and career readiness support, disabled Veterans affirmative action program,

			and human resources support.
		(404) 929-3152	**The Vocational Rehabilitation & Employment Service (VR&E)**
			VetSuccess Program assists Veterans with service-connected disabilities to prepare for, find, and keep suitable jobs. For Veterans with Service-Connected Disabilities so severe that they cannot immediately consider work, VetSuccess offers services to improve their ability to live as independently as possible. Trying to Make Broader Decisions About Your Career? American Corporate Partners (ACP)* is a nationwide mentoring program dedicated to helping recently returned Veterans transition to the civilian workforce through mentoring, career counseling, and networking. Combat to Corporate* is a website developed by a Veteran that helps explain how to apply your military training to succeed and excel in the business world. — See more at: http://www.va.gov/VETSINWORKPLA CE/careerfields.asp#sthash.9M9qbFbi .dpuf
Goodwill-VET SUCCESS Program	Veterans Round tables are ongoing at: -Duluth, -Northeast Plaza, -Smyrna, and -Woodstock.	678-891-0235 770) 874-0901	**also inquire about their Vet support groups** VET SUCCESS helps veterans transition into the workplace. We don't just get you any job—we find one that fits your unique skills. Whether you're looking for full-time or temporary employment, we've placed veterans in both blue- and white-collar positions, including logistics, construction, maintenance, manufacturing, security, and a whole lot more. For veterans with disabilities, Goodwill offers a range of programs and support specifically designed to meet your needs. We also have relationships with employers, US Department of Veteran Affairs - Vocational Rehabilitation and Employment
Dekalb Workforce Development	774 Jordan Lane, Bldg #4,	(404) 687-3400	www.dekalbworkforce.org

	Decatur, GA 30033		
Atlanta Workforce Development Agency	818 Pollard Blvd SW, Atlanta, GA 30315	(404) 658-9675	http://www.atlantaga.gov/index.aspx?page=889
Georgia Department of Labor (DOL) Career Centers	Vet Outreach Specialist	(404) 699-6900 (404) 679-5200 (678) 479-5886 (770) 840-2200 (770) 784-2455 (770) 784-4064 (770) 528-6100	2636-14 Martin Luther King, Jr. Dr., Atlanta, GA 30311 (S. Metro Atlanta) 2943 N. Druid Hills Rd., Atlanta, GA 30329 (N. Metro Atlanta) 2450 Mt. Zion Pkwy, Suite 100, Jonesboro, GA 30236 (Clayton) 2211 Beaver Ruin Rd., Suite 160 Norcross, GA 30071 (Gwinnett) 7249 Industrial Blvd, NE Covington, GA 30014-1499 (Newton, Jasper, Walton) 465 Big Shanty Rd., Marietta, GA 30066 (Cobb, Cherokee)
Financial Resources			
Supplemental Nutrition Assistance Program (SNAP)		Call 877-423-4746 and asking that an application be mailed to you Or Request this application be printed directly from the Social Worker giving you this information ☺	SNAP offers nutrition assistance to millions of eligible, low-income individuals and families and provides economic benefits to communities. SNAP is the largest program in the domestic hunger safety net. The Food and Nutrition Service works with State agencies, nutrition educators, and neighborhood and faith-based organizations to ensure that those eligible for nutrition assistance can make informed decisions about applying for the program and can access benefits.
Veterans of Foreign Wars (VFW) National Military Services		http://www.vfw.org/UnmetNeeds/ Contact Unmet Needs at 1-866-789-6333 or by email at unmetneeds@vfw.org	Unmet Needs is there to help America's service members who have been deployed in the last six years and have run into unexpected financial difficulties as a result of one of the following • Deployment • Military pay issue • Military illness or injury Applicants can receive funds only once every 18 months, and only

		with any questions.	twice total; all grants are paid directly to the creditor and not to the applicant. Second requests for assistance must be caused by a new situation or deployment. Housing expenses – mortgage, rent, repairs, insurance ☐ Vehicle expenses – payments, insurance, repairs ☐ Utilities and primary phone ☐ Food and incidentals ☐ Children's clothing, diapers, formula, necessary school or childcare expenses ☐ Medical bills, prescriptions & eyeglasses – the patient's portion for necessary or emergency medical care only
USA Cares Inc.		http://www.usacares.org/ 800) 773-0387	The USA Cares staff, board of directors and volunteers want to thank you for your dedicated service to our country. Please know that we will do everything we can to assist you in your time of need, whether it is through mentoring, referral or financial support. At USA Cares we assist: Post-9/11,OIF/OEF service members, veterans and their family members who are in financial crisis due to military service or circumstances beyond all personal control Typically, USA Cares provides assistance in four major areas: -**Emergency Assistance**—utilities, food, etc. -**Housing Assistance** – prevent evictions and foreclosures -Combat Injured, to include the invisible wounds of post-traumatic stress (PTS) and traumatic brain injury (TBI) -**Jobs Assistance** – reduce unemployment among post-9/11 Veterans
Operation Homefront		3375 Chastain Gardens Drive, Unit 160 Kennesaw, GA	KEY SERVICES: By connecting the American donor community to our military families

168

		30144 Phone: (770) 575-2086 Emergency Assistance: (877) 264-3968 http://www.operationhomefront.net/	through a robust array of valued and life-changing programs that address the specific short-term and critical assistance, long-term stability and recurring support needs they experience, Operation Homefront is able to help military families overcome many of the challenges inherent in military life. The result: stronger, more stable and more secure military families. Our programs include: **SHORT-TERM AND CRITICAL ASSISTANCE** □ Financial assistance* for food, utilities, home repairs, rent/mortgage payments, etc. □ Rent-free transitional housing for wounded service members □ Operation Homefront assists military families during difficult financial times by providing food assistance, auto and home repair, vision care, travel and transportation, moving assistance, essential home items, and financial assistance **LONG-TERM STABILITY** □ Mortgage-free homes awarded across the U.S. **ONGOING FAMILY SUPPORT** □ Hearts of Valor caregiver support program □ Baby showers to help new military moms welcome the newest member of the family □ Homefront Celebrations to recognize military spouses □ Holiday programs to provide meals and toys □ Backpacks filled with school supplies for military kids *Emergency financial assistance is in the form of checks paid directly to mortgage lenders, auto mechanics, contractors, hospitals, doctors, and other providers.
Housing Resources			
United Way of Greater Atlanta	100 Edgewood Avenue, N.E.	**Phone:** 404-527-7200	**Our solutions focus on housing the chronically homeless and helping them address the issues that led to their**

	Atlanta, Georgia 30303	**Email:** info@unitedwayatlanta.org	**homelessness.** • Services Include • Street-to-Home • Hospital-to-Home • Securing of benefits • Case management • Job training • Connection to VA homeless services • ARCH – Assistance in Re-housing Chronically Homeless Veterans • Transitional housing w/ case management
Homeless Veterans Program	Fort McPherson 1701 Hardee Ave., SW Atlanta, GA 30330	404-321-6111 Ext. 7284 or 6900 Be sure to Ask about the following programs.	If you're a Veteran, you may be connected with the Homeless Program point of contact at the nearest VA facility. Contact information will be requested so staff may follow up. The **Homeless Veteran Supported Employment Program (HVSEP)** provides vocational assistance, job development and placement, and ongoing supports to improve employment outcomes among homeless Veterans and Veterans at-risk of homelessness. Formerly homeless Veterans who have been trained as Vocational Rehabilitation Specialists (VRSs) provide these services. VA's **Compensated Work VA's Therapy (CWT)** is comprised of three unique programs which assist homeless Veterans in returning to competitive employment: Sheltered Workshop, Transitional Work, and Supported Employment. Veterans in CWT are paid at least the federal or state minimum wage, whichever is higher Veterans are screened by the physician/psychiatrist prior to admission into the TR house. Veterans must receive a complete H&P examination by a qualified health provider and be medically cleared for admission. Baseline

			labs are ordered on all Veterans participating in the MH RRTP.
			HUD-VA Supportive Housing (VASH) Program is a joint effort between the Department of Housing and Urban Development and VA. HUD allocated nearly 38,000 "Housing Choice" Section 8 vouchers across the country. These vouchers allow Veterans and their families to live in market rate rental units while VA provides case management services. A housing subsidy is paid to the landlord on behalf of the participating Veteran. The Veteran then pays the difference between the actual rent charged by the landlord and the amount subsidized by the program. Learn more about the HUD-VASH Program
		404-321-6111, ext. 7436	The central goal of the **Health Care for Homeless Veterans (HCHV)** program is to reduce homelessness among Veterans by reaching out to those who are the most vulnerable and engaging them in supportive and rehabilitative services. Outreach services are also provided through Community Resource and Referral Centers (CRRCs), located in many large urban areas, and at Stand Down events. CRRCs offer Veterans who are homeless or at risk of homelessness with one-stop access to multiple VA and community resources at a single location. VA and community partners are on hand to provide immediate assistance and/or referral services.
Legal Resources			
Voluntary Service	Atlanta VAMC	404) 321-6111 x7728 Mr. Franchi Clark	Offers Veterans a free legal consultation with Legal advocate from the community- CALL TO SCHEDULE APPT.

State Bar of Georgia		Norman Zoller 404-527-8765 normanz@gabar.org	The State Bar of Georgia Military Legal Assistance Program assists service members and veterans by connecting them to State Bar members who are willing to provide free or reduced-fee legal services. Service members and veterans often have legal needs in their personal lives and specific to their military service. They also face financial issues and other civil law matters resulting from the sacrifices made in military life. Depending on eligibility, clients will be connected to a lawyer in their geographic area with expertise in their area of need.
Georgia Law Center for the Homeless	100 Edgewood Avenue Atlanta, GA 30303	404-681-0680 404-681-0681 Jcorrea@galawcenter.org	Needs: Disability, Family & Juvenile, Homeless, Housing, Public Benefits, Veterans
Atlanta Legal Aid Society	To apply, call the county office where you live, or one of our special intake units. **IMPORTANT: Call for intake hours before visiting.** http://www.georgialegalaid.org/ for more info on understanding your legal issue or how to find help	Clayton/South Fulton 777 Cleveland Avenue, SW, Ste 410 Atlanta, GA 30315 (404) 669-0233 Cobb 30 South Park Square Marietta, GA 30090 (770) 528-2565 DeKalb 246 Sycamore Street Decatur, GA 30030-3434 (404) 377-0701 Fulton 54 Ellis Street NE Atlanta, GA 30303	Atlanta Legal Aid Society helps low-income people meet basic needs through free civil legal services. Last year, our attorneys handled more than 20,000 cases helping over 50,000 people in metro Atlanta meet some of life's most basic needs — a safe home, enough food to eat, a decent education, protection against fraud, and personal safety. Our clients have annual incomes below 200% of the federal poverty limit — about $23,000 for an individual or $48,000 for a family of four, and they come from Clayton, Cobb, DeKalb, Fulton, and Gwinnett counties. Our offices are located in downtown Atlanta, East Point, Decatur, Marietta, and Lawrenceville, as well as through our Health Law Partnership where attorneys are housed at Scottish Rite, Egleston and Hughes Spalding children's hospitals.

		(404) 524-5811	
		Gwinnett 324 West Pike Street Lawrenceville, GA 30046 (678) 376-4545 *directions* Health Law Partnership (HeLP) Main Office 975 Johnson Ferry Road, Suite 360 Atlanta, GA 30342 (404) 785-2005 *directions*	
Atlanta Volunteer Lawyers Foundation, Inc.	235 Peachtree St, NE Suite 1750 North Tower Atlanta, GA 30303	404-521-0790 http://www.avlf.o rg	Needs: Consumer,Debt/Credit/Bankruptcy ,Education,Employment,Family & Juvenile,Foreclosure,Homeless, Housing,Public Benefits,Taxes Domestic Violence
Augusta Regional Office, Georgia Legal Services Program«	209 7th Street, 4th Floor Augusta, GA 30903-2185	404-721-2327 http://www.glsp. org Needs:	Consumer,Education,Elder Law,Employment,Family & Juvenile,Foreclosure,Housing, Life Planning,Public Benefits,Veterans
Cobb Justice Foundation	30 South Park Square Marietta, GA 30090	(770) 528-2565 http://www.cobbj ustice.org/	Needs: Consumer,Debt/Credit/Bankruptcy ,Disability,Education,Elder Law,Employment,Family & Juvenile,Foreclosure,Health,Home less,Housing,Life Planning,Public Benefits,Veterans Protective Orders for Domestic Violence Victims
Columbus Regional Office, Georgia Legal Services Program«	1036 First Avenue Columbus, GA 31902	706-649-7493 http://www.glsp. org	Needs: Community Development,Consumer,Debt/Cre dit/Bankruptcy,Education,Elder Law,Employment,Family & Juvenile,Foreclosure,Health,Home less,Housing,Life Planning,Public Benefits,Veterans
Gainesville Regional Office,	705 Washington Street NW Suite	770-535-5717 http://www.glsp.	Needs: Consumer, Debt/Credit/Bankruptcy,Education,

Georgia Legal Services Program	B-1 Gainesville, GA 30501	org	Elder Law,Employment,Family & Juvenile,Foreclosure,Health,Home less,Housing,Life Planning,Public Benefits,Veterans

For these Depts., call the main Atlanta VAMC phone number: 404-321-6111 and the clinic extension

RHEUMATOLOGY	EXTENSION: 2074
PODIATRY	EXTENSION: 6519
NEPHROLOGY	EXTENSION: 7070
INFECTIOUS DISEASE	EXTENSION: 7748
GASTRENTEROLOGY	EXTENSION: 6630
ENDOCRINOLOGY	EXTENSION: 2069
DIABETES EDUCATION	EXTENSION: 2075
DERMATOLOGY	EXTENSION: 6380
CARDIOLOGY	EXTENSION: 6190
ULTRASOUND/CT SCAN	EXTENSION: 6718
PROSTHETICS	EXTENSION: 2015
EYE CLINIC	EXTENSION: 6660
AUDIOLOGY	EXTENSION: 6515 OR 6520
HEMATOLOGY	EXTENSION: 7680
NEUROLOGY	EXTENSION: 7171 OR 3077
ORTHOPEDICS	EXTENSION: 6600

VETERAN TRANSPORTATION SERVICES:

IF YOU RESIDE WITHIN A 30 MILE RADIUS OF THE MAIN HOSPITAL LOCATION, THE AUSTEL CBOC, THE LAWRENCEVILLE CBOC, THE STOCKBRIDGE CBOC OR THE EAST POINT/FORT MCPHERSON CBOC:
- CALL: 404-728-4190 AND PRESS OPTION # 2
  OR
  404-321-6111 x7533
- YOU MUST CALL 7 DAYS BEFORE YOUR APPOINTMENT

DAV Transportation   404-321-6111 Ext. 7715

MEDICATION REFILLS CAN BE OBTAINED BY CALLING:
404-235-3084
404- 235-3087
1800-370-8387

SUBSTANCE ABUSE PROGRAM (SATP/ESP):

The hours for open access intake are between 7:00 AM and 9:00 AM. Please present as early as possible as the intake line can sometimes be long.

Please present to the SATP Program within three business days of the day your consult is placed. Your consult will be discontinued after that and you will not be able to be seen as a walk in patient.

The hours for open access intake are between 7:00 AM and 9:00 AM. Please present as early as possible as the intake line can sometimes be long.

If you are not able to present for a walk-in intake assessment during the open access hours, please call the SATP Program at (404)-321-6111 ext. 6900 to schedule an intake appointment. Please be mindful to place the CALL to schedule your intake

13

appointment within three business days of the day your consult is placed. You appointment may be scheduled for a later date, as long as your call is made within the stated time frame.

The SATP Program is located in Modular Building #2 (behind the VA Community Living Center - Nursing Home). When you enter the VA Main Campus follow the road all the way to the left. The modular buildings are located in front of parking deck F and next to building D.

VA PATIENT ADVOCATES OFFICE

Our Patient Advocate program seeks to personally give you and your family the security of knowing someone is available to focus on your individual concerns and rights as a patient. We work directly with all departments on your behalf and can address your questions, problems or special needs quicker. If you, or a veteran you care for has not been able to resolve important issues related to VA through other means of communications, please contact one of our highly-skilled patient advocates listed below who will be eager to help you with your concern in a timely manner. "We're Here to Help!"
No Patient Advocates listed.

Located in the Main VAMC: Room 1B152, Phone: 404.321.6111 Extensions: 3051/2264, Hours of Operation: Monday – Friday 8:00 a.m. 4:30 p.m.

Also located in the Atlanta CBOC and the Ft. McPherson CBOC

You can also call this office for "Person in Charge" contact information for the department or clinic of your VA care experience, to express your general concerns and/or suggestions.

MILITARY EXPOSURES

Veterans may have been exposed to a range of environmental and chemical hazards during military service including sand, dust, and particulates; burn pits; infectious diseases; and other hazards. VA offers several programs and resources related to military exposure concerns for non-VA providers and Veterans that are not receiving care through VA's health care system. The following are a few examples of resources that you can share with your non-VA health care provider.

The Burn Pit Registry: What You Need to Know

In 2014, VA launched the Airborne Hazards and Open Burn Pit Registry for Veterans and Servicemembers who were exposed to open air burn pits at military sites in Iraq and Afghanistan. It contains health information collected from thousands of Veterans and active duty Servicemembers who completed a questionnaire online. VA is studying the health of exposed Veterans and Servicemembers through the Burn Pit Registry and other research efforts. If you are a Veteran or Servicemember who served in eligible locations you can participate in the Burn Pit Registry. Even if you do not have any current symptoms, VA encourages you to take part.

Here's what you need to know about the Burn Pit Registry:

1. The Burn Pit Registry tells VA about your exposures. By completing an online questionnaire, Veterans and Servicemembers can use the Burn Pit Registry to report their exposures and related health concerns, and to document their health. As the long-term effects of exposure to airborne hazards during service are still relatively unknown, documenting exposures early ensures that participants will be monitored over time and that VA can improve programs to provide the necessary health care and resources should any health problems emerge. Burn Pit Registry Key Findings (click image to see full infographic)

2. The registry provides a summary of your health for you and your health care providers. The Burn Pit Registry helps participants to become more aware of their own health and allows them to receive updates about ongoing VA studies and

14

treatments. It also helps researchers to study the health effects of burn pits and other airborne hazards, resulting in better long-term health care from VA for current and future Veterans and Servicemembers. Those who are eligible can get an optional, no-cost, in-person medical evaluation.

3. Many Veterans who deployed after 1990 are eligible to join the registry. VA uses deployment information from the Department of Defense (DoD) to determine eligibility for the Burn Pit Registry. To be eligible, you must be a Veteran or Servicemember who served in the Southwest Asia theater of operations at any time on or after August 2, 1990, or Afghanistan or Djibouti on or after September 11, 2001. This includes the following countries, bodies of water, and the airspace above these locations:

- Iraq
- Afghanistan
- Kuwait
- Saudi Arabia
- Bahrain
- Djibouti
- Gulf of Aden
- Gulf of Oman
- Oman
- Qatar
- United Arab Emirates
- Waters of the Persian Gulf, Arabian Sea, and Red Sea

4. Sign up for the Burn Pit Registry in three easy steps. To sign up for the Burn Pit Registry, visit https://veteran.mobilehealth.va.gov/AHBurnPitRegistry .
  - Step 1: Make sure you have a DoD Self-Service Level 2 Logon (Premium DS Logon Level 2) account. If you don't already have one, you can apply for a DS Logon account at https://myaccess.dmdc.osd.mil. While a Premium DS Logon Level 2 account is required to access the registry at this time, VA is exploring other ways to access the registry website in the future.
  - Step 2: Complete and submit the online questionnaire. The questionnaire takes about 40 minutes to complete. You can complete it all at once, or log out and return later.

  - Step 3: Print and save your completed questionnaire for your records. You can use your completed questionnaire when talking to a health care provider about your exposures.

5. Technical support is available for the registry. **Call the Registry Help Desk at 1-877-470-5947 from Monday through Friday 8 AM to 8 PM** to get questions answered and for help with any technical problems you might experience while registering. Frequently asked questions and answers about the registry are also available at https://veteran.mobilehealth.va.gov/AHBurnPitRegistry/index.html#page/faq . To learn more about burn pits and burn pit research, visit www.publichealth.va.gov/exposures/burnpits/index.asp.

For more information on the Burn Pit Registry, and to sign up, visit https://veteran.mobilehealth.va.gov/AHBurnPitRegistry . Join the Registry All eligible Veterans and Servicemembers who were exposed to airborne hazards during deployment are encouraged to participate in the registry. Even if you're not showing any symptoms, your participation is important. Help improve health awareness and long-term health for you and all Veterans—join the registry today.

Exposure to Chemical Warfare Agents

Servicemembers who handled or demolished explosive ordnances during Operation Iraqi Freedom (OIF) and Operation New Dawn (OND) may have been exposed to chemical warfare agents (CWAs) and may experience related health effects. While Explosive Ordnance Disposal (EOD) personnel are most likely to have been exposed, non-EOD personnel may have also been exposed during Improvised Explosive Device (IED) attacks or during the open air demolition or transport of CWAs.

CWAs are toxic chemicals used as a method of warfare, such as mustard agents or sarin. A list of CWAs may be found on Schedule 1 of the Chemical Weapons Convention. Research on the long-term health effects of exposure to CWAs is limited, but VA is collaborating with the Department of Defense (DoD) to better understand the potential health effects.

15

VA and DoD are currently working together to identify and contact active duty Servicemembers and Veterans who may have been exposed to CWAs during OIF and OND. To date, approximately 7,000 Servicemembers with possible exposure have been identified.

If you believe you may have been exposed to CWAs and have not been contacted, please call the DoD hotline at 1-800-497-6261. **VA and DoD would like to ensure that your exposures are documented, and that you are aware of any related health care benefits.**

Have you completed your free gulf war registry exam?

If you served during OIF or OND you are eligible to receive a free, in-person VA Gulf War Registry exam. To make an appointment, contact your local Environmental Health Coordinator:

Leatrice McGrew-Britten Atlanta VAMC
(404) 321-6111 x2181
Leatrice.McGrew-Britten@va.gov

Atlanta VA Medical Center
1670 Clairmont Rd.
Atlanta, GA 30033

The Gulf War Registry is a helpful tool for Veterans and researchers. It is a way for Veterans to learn about the possible health effects of exposure to environmental hazards, and helps VA improve care for those health effects. To learn more, visit www.publichealth.va.gov/exposures/gulfwar/benefits/registry-exam.asp. You may also be eligible to participate in VA's Airborne Hazards and Open Burn Pit Registry. By completing an online questionnaire, you can report your exposures and related health concerns.

Community Based Outpatient Clinics (CBOCs)

Atlanta VA Clinic **(formerly the Decatur Clinic)** 250 N. Arcadia Ave. Decatur, GA 30030 (404) 417-5200 (404) 417-5204 Fax Hours of Operation: 7:30am-3:00pm Mon-Thurs 7:30am-12:00pm Fri (Lab Entrance Hours the same)	**Lawrenceville Clinic** 455 Philip Blvd., Ste 200 Lawrenceville, GA 30046 (404) 417-1750 (404) 417-1708 Fax Hours of Operation: 7:00am-4:00pm Mon-Thurs 7:30am-12:00pm Fri	**Gwinnett County Clinic** **(formerly MH North)** 1970 Riverside Pkwy. Lawrenceville, GA 30043 (404) 329-2222 (678) 376-0598 Fax Hours of Operation: 7:00am-4:00pm Mon-Thurs 7:30am-12:00pm Fri
NE GA/Oakwood Clinic 4175 Tanners Creek Dr. Oakwood, GA 30566 (404) 728-8210 (404) 728-8229 Fax Hours of Operation: 8:00am-4:00pm Mon-Thurs 8:00am-12:00pm Fri	**Blairsville Clinic** 1294 Highway 515 East Suite 100 Blairsville, GA 30512 (404) 329-2222 Hours of Operation: 7:30am-3:30pm Mon-Fri Lab Entrance 7:30am-2:00pm Mon-Fri **TAP Line – (404) 329-4650**	**Rome Clinic** 30 Chateau Dr. SE Rome, GA 30161 (706) 235-6581 (706) 291-3753 Fax Hours of Operation: 8:00am-6:00pm Mon, Tues, Thur, Fri
Carrollton Clinic 180 Martin Drive Carrollton, GA 30117 (404) 329-2222 Hours of Operation: 7:30am-5:00pm Mon-Fri **TAP Line – (404) 728-7627**	**Newnan Clinic** 39-A Oak Hill Ct. Newnan, GA 30265 (404) 329-2222 (404) 417-2910 Fax Hours of Operation: 7:30am-3:30pm Mon-Fri **TAP Line – (404) 728-5071**	**Austell Clinic** 2041 Mesa Valley Way Austell, GA 30082 (404) 417-1760 (404) 417-1770 Fax Hours of Operation: 7:30am-3:30pm Mon-Fri **TAP Line – (404) 217-2150**
Ft. McPherson Clinic **(formerly East Point CBOC)** 1701 Hardee Ave SW Atlanta, GA 30310 (404) 329-2222 (404) 327-4948 Fax Hours of Operation: 8:00am-4:00pm Mon-Thurs 8:00am-12:00pm Fri	**Stockbridge Clinic** 175 Medical Blvd. (Near Henry Medical Center) Stockbridge, GA 30281 (404) 329-2209 (404) 728-5096 Fax Hours of Operation: 7:30am-4:00pm Mon-Fri **TAP Line – (404) 728-5099**	

Applying For Benefits

Veterans Benefits Administration (VBA)- Atlanta Regional Office	1700 Clairmont Road Atlanta, GA 30033	1(800) 827-1000 http://www.vba.va.gov/pubs/forms/VBA-21-526EZ-ARE.pdf	The Veterans Benefits Administration (VBA) provides a variety of benefits and services to Servicemembers, Veterans, and their families.
Compensation and Pension	Fulton County Clinic	404-321-6111 Ext. 1900	
VSO OFFICES: Benefits/Claims Assistance- *"Advocacy Offices"*			
Georgia Department of Veterans Service	Atlanta VAMC VAMC 1st floor between the Credit Union and Radiology	(404) 321-6111 x6359 or x6357 Or Garner Bracey 404-728-7611	State of Georgia Department of Veterans Services is available to assist with ongoing benefit related needs and for advocacy or help should you want to submit additional claims or appeals. There is an office in the Atlanta VAMC on the first floor by the credit union **and there are also field offices. Request if needed.**
Disabled American Veterans (DAV)	1700 Clairmont Road Atlanta, GA 30033	404-929-5956	Providing free, professional assistance to veterans and your families in obtaining benefits and services earned through military service and provided by the Department of Veterans Affairs (VA) and other agencies of government.

About eBenefits

Welcome to eBenefits! This site is the result of a collaboration between the Department of Veterans Affairs (VA) and the Department of Defense (DoD). We serve Veterans, Service members, Wounded Warriors, their family members, and their authorized caregivers. **This account can be used to manage and access your personal information and benefits record information.**

What We Offer You

- A secure environment where you can safely access your personal information and perform self-service tasks.

- Applications (online and PDF) for disability compensation and various benefits.

- Employment resources.

- A personalized Dashboard that you can customize to suit your preferences and information needs.

- Access to the National Resource Directory, which enables you to find links to resource based on subjects that interest you.

Levels of Access

To gain access to most eBenefits resources and services, you need an account. We offer the following two types of account, and both of them are free:

- A Basic account that gives you limited access to various features.

- A Premium account that gives you unlimited access.

To register for your free account, you need a DS Logon

Contact By Phone

eBenefits Questions and Technical Issues

1-800-983-0937

Monday - Friday, 8:00 am - 8:00 pm ET

A WARRIOR MARRIED TO HIS WIFE AND PTSD

There are numerous ways to apply for VA benefits depending on the type of benefit you are seeking.

Benefits	How To Apply
Before Leaving Military Service – Pre-Discharge Program for Servicemembers	If you are a member of the armed forces serving on either active duty or full-time National Guard duty, you should apply through the VA Pre-Discharge Program before leaving service.
VA Work-Study Department	The student must complete a **VA Form 22-8691**, *Application for Work-Study Allowance,* and submit it through the Site Supervisor to the VA Work-Study Department via email or fax. Once the application is received and approved by VA, a contract and time record will be emailed to the Site Supervisor. The contract is to be signed by the student, and the signed contract returned to VA by the Site Supervisor via email or fax. Students may submit an application for work-study benefits up to 45 days before their qualifying school term starts. However, they must be sure the school has submitted their enrollment for the same term.
Vocational Rehabilitation and Employment Benefits for Servicemembers and Veterans	The best way to file for vocational rehabilitation and employment services is to apply online at eBenefits.va.gov. If you don't have an eBenefits account, register today. In eBenefits, apply using the Veterans On-line Application (VONAPP) to complete and submit your application online. The form to use is called VA Form 28-1900, "Disabled Veterans Application for Vocational Rehabilitation." Download VA Form 28-1900 You can also mail the VA Form 28-1900, "Disabled Veterans Application for Vocational Rehabilitation" to your local regional benefit office. You can locate your local regional benefit office using the VA Facility Locator. You may also visit your local regional benefit office and turn in your application for processing. Visit Vocational Rehabilitation & Employment for more information on vocational rehabilitation and employment services.
Disability Compensation Benefits for Veterans	The best way to file for disability compensation is to apply online at eBenefits.va.gov. If you don't have an eBenefits account, register today. Once you log into your eBenefits account, use Apply for Disability Compensation. VA recommends you appoint an accredited Veterans Service Officer to help you initiate your claim, gather the required medical records and evidence, and submit your claim. You can appoint a Veteran Service Officer while you apply online. If you prefer to file your claim by paper, complete VA Form 21-526EZ, "Application for Disability Compensation and Related Compensation Benefits" and mail the application to your local regional benefit office. You can find your local regional benefit office in the VA

	Facility Locator. You can also visit your local regional office and turn in your application for processing. While there, you can appoint an accredited Veterans Service Officer to help you prepare and submit your claim. You can find an accredited Veteran Service Officer using eBenefits. **Download VA Form 21-526EZ** Visit Applying for Compensation for more information on how to apply for compensation.
Dependency and Indemnity Compensation Benefits for Survivors and Dependents	Download and complete VA Form 21-534EZ, "Application for DIC, Death Pension, and/or Accrued Benefits" and mail it to your local regional benefit office. You can locate your local regional benefit office using the VA Facility Locator. You may also visit your local regional benefit office and turn in your application for processing. We recommend that you appoint an accredited Veterans Service Officer to help you initiate your claim and gather any required medical records or evidence. You can find an accredited Veteran Service Officer using eBenefits. **Download VA Form 21-534EZ** If the death was in service, your Military Casualty Assistance Officer will assist you in completing VA Form 21-534a, "Application for Dependency and Indemnity Compensation, Death Pension and Accrued Benefits by a Surviving Spouse or Child" and in mailing the application to the Philadelphia Regional Benefit Office. **Download VA Form 21-534a** Visit Dependency and Indemnity Compensation for more information on compensation benefits for survivors and dependents.
Pension Benefits for Veterans	Download and complete VA Form 21-527EZ, "Application for Pension." You can mail your application to your local regional benefit office. You can locate your local regional benefit office using the VA Facility Locator. You may also visit your local regional benefit office and turn in your application for processing. **Download VA Form 21-527EZ** VA recommends you appoint an accredited Veterans Service Officer to help you initiate your claim and gather any required medical records or evidence. You can find an accredited Veteran Service Officer using eBenefits. Visit Veterans Pension or more information on Veterans Pension benefits,.
Pension Benefits for Survivors	Download and complete VA Form 21-534EZ, "Application for DIC, Death Pension, and/or Accrued Benefits" and mail it to your local regional benefit office. You can locate your local regional benefit office using the VA Facility Locator. You may also visit your local regional benefit office and turn in your application for processing.

	Download VA Form 21-534EZ VA recommends you appoint an accredited Veterans Service Officer to help you initiate your claim and gather any required medical records or evidence. You can find an accredited Veteran Service Officer using eBenefits. For more information on Survivors Pension benefits, visit the Survivors Pension web page.
Education Benefits for Veterans	You can apply for your education benefits using eBenefits.va.gov. If you don't have an eBenefits account, register today. In eBenefits, apply using the Veterans On-line Application (VONAPP) to complete and submit your application online. You can also submit a paper application. To do this, download and complete VA Form 22-1990, "Application for VA Education Benefits" and mail it to a VA Regional Processing Office. You can mail the form to the region of your home address or to the VA Regional Processing Office for the region of your school's physical address, if you know what school you want to attend. Also, you can call a VA Education Case Manager (1-888-GIBill1) to ask for help. **Download VA Form 22-1990** For more information on how to apply online, visit the Education Apply for Benefits web page.
Home Loan Benefits for Servicemembers and Veterans	You can apply for a home loan certificate of eligibility online using ebenefits.va.gov. You may also apply for a home loan certificate of eligibility through your lender. To apply by mail, use VA Form 26-1880, "Request for Certificate of Eligibility." **Download VA Form 26-1880** You can mail the application to: VA Loan Eligibility Center Attn: COE (262) PO Box 100034 Decatur, GA 30031 For more information on eligibility, evidence, and how to apply, visit the Certificate of Eligibility web page.
Home Loan Benefits for Survivors	The surviving spouse of a Servicemember or Veteran must apply by mail. The form to complete is the VA Form 26-1817, "Request for Determination of Loan Guaranty Eligibility - Unmarried Surviving Spouses." Or, you can call 1-888-768-2132 and follow the prompts for Eligibility and we will mail the form to you. **Download VA Form 26-1817**

	Mail your application to this address: VA Loan Eligibility Center Attn: COE (262) PO Box 100034 Decatur, GA 30031 For more information on eligibility, evidence, and how to apply, visit the Certificate of Eligibility web page.
Life Insurance Benefits for Servicemembers, Veterans, and Survivors	**Servicemembers' Group Life Insurance (SGLI):** SGLI coverage is automatic. You do not need to apply. To designate beneficiaries, or reduce, decline or restore SGLI coverage, complete and submit SGLV 8286, "Servicemembers' Group Life Insurance Election and Certificate" to your branch of service personnel clerk. **Download Form SGLV 8286** Visit Servicemembers' Group Life Insurance for more information on Servicemembers' Group Life Insurance,. **Veterans' Group Life Insurance(VGLI):** To file for VGLI, you can apply online using eBenefits.va.gov. If you don't have an eBenefits account, register today. You may also download and complete SGLV 8714, "Application for Veterans' Group Life Insurance." **Download Form SGLV 8714** Mail your application to this address: OSGLI PO Box 41618 Philadelphia, PA 19176-9913 Visit Veterans' Group Life Insurance for more information on Veterans' Group Life Insurance, . **Family Servicemembers' Group Life Insurance (FSGLI):** To decline, reduce, or restore FSGLI coverage, complete and file form SGLV 8286A, "Spouse Coverage Election and Certificate" with your branch of service. **Download Form SGLV 8286A** Visit Family Servicemembers' Life Group Insurance for more information on Family Servicemembers' Group Life Insurance. **Servicemembers' Group Life Insurance Traumatic Injury Protection Program (TSGLI):** To file a claim for TSGLI, complete and file SGLV 8600, "Application for TSGLI Benefits" with your branch of service. Coverage for this benefit is automatic for all

Servicemembers covered by SGLI.

Download Form SGLV 8600

Visit the Servicemembers' Group Life Insurance Traumatic Injury Protection Program for more information on the Servicemembers' Group Life Insurance Traumatic Injury Protection Program,.

Service-Disabled Veterans' Insurance (S-DVI): To file for S-DVI, apply online using the online policy access page or complete VA Form 29-4364, "Application for Service-Disabled Veterans' Insurance."

Download VA Form 29-4364

Mail your application to this address:

Department of Veterans Affairs Regional Office and Insurance Center (RH)
P.O. Box 7208
Philadelphia, PA 19101

Visit Service-Disabled Veterans' Insurance for more information on Service-Disabled Veterans' Insurance,.

Veterans' Mortgage Life Insurance (VMLI): To file for VMLI, complete and submit VA Form 29-8636, "Application for Veterans' Mortgage Life Insurance" to your Specially Adapted Housing Agent. The agent will help you complete your application. Also, you must provide information about your current mortgage.

Download VA Form 29-8636

Visit Veterans' Mortgage Life Insurance for more information on Veterans' Mortgage Life Insurance, .

CURTIS BUTLER III

** VBA BENEFITS LISTED THAT ARE AVAILABLE FOR SERVICE CONNECTED DISABLED VETERANS

You qualify services for everything between 0%- YOUR SC Rating %

0% SC and Higher

- Home loan Guaranty Certificate of Eligibility
- Service Disabled Veterans Life Insurance. Must file within 2 years from initial notice of Service connected disability. ($10,000 of insurance only)
- Outpatient treatment for: (1) service connected conditions, and (2) for all medical conditions if enrolled in VA healthcare program. Co-payment for treatment may apply for non-service connected conditions.
- Travel allowance for scheduled appointment for care of service connected conditions at VA Medical Centers, and out-patient clinics. (Eligibility based on the distance traveled of 25 miles or more or a veteran's income.)
- Medical treatment for any condition: Enrollment in a VA health care program is encouraged but not required for treatment of a service connected condition. (A co-payment will apply for treatment of non-service connected conditions, and prescription drugs)
- Prosthetic Devices: for service connected conditions, to include but not limited too wheelchairs, canes, crutches, hospital beds, Nebulizer, oxygen tanks, and electric scooters, the issue of any prosthetic devices requires a VA Doctors prescription.
- Medical Treatment in non-VA facilities for service connected conditions with an authorized fee-basis card issued by the VA Medical Center. (Certain restrictions apply.)
- Ten Point Civil Service Preference (10 points added to Civil Service test score only after veterans achieves at least 70 on a test.)
- Annual Clothing Allowance of $586.00 for veterans with a service connected condition that requires the use of a prosthetic or orthopedic appliance (artificial limbs, braces, wheelchairs) or use prescribed medications for a skin condition which tend to wear, tear, or soil clothing. The items used must be prescribed and dispensed at a VA Medical Center.
- Temporary ratings of 100%, based on the hospitalization for a service connected disability requiring at least one month of convalescence or immobilization by cast.
- Dental treatment for: (1) service connected dental condition, or (2) follow-up dental treatment which has begun while hospitalized at a VA Medical Center, or any former Prisoner of War with 90 consecutive days or more of confinement. Some restrictions may apply.
- Home Improvement and Structural Alteration Grant Program: Administered by the Prosthetics Depart at VA Medical Facilities. For medically required improvements and/or structural changes to the veteran's residence. This Grant requires a VA Doctor's prescription. Service connected veterans can receive up too a $4,100 grant. Non-Service connected veterans may receive a grant up to $1,200. The grant is to be used for allowing entrance or exit improvements for residence, essential lavatory and sanitary facilities, kitchen and bathroom accessibility to sinks and counters. This grant is not for complete remodeling of a veterans bath or kitchen.

10-20% SC and Higher, all of the above plus:

- Vocational Rehabilitation which includes full medical and dental care, a substance allowance in addition to disability payments, payment for all required school related supplies and direct payment of tuition.
- Funding Fee waived for Home loan Guaranty loans.

30% SC and Higher, all of the above plus:

- Addition compensation for dependents (Spouse, children, adopted children, and dependent parents)
- Non-Competitive Civil Service appointment: Job appointment without the requirement of an interview.

186

- Affirmative action in employment: A disabled veteran cannot be passed over to hire a non-disabled veteran or non-veteran unless at least three interviews have been conducted by the employer.
- Additional allowance for a spouse who is a patient in a nursing home: (Helpless or blind, or so nearly helpless as to require the aid and attendance of another person.)

40% SC and Higher, all of the above plus:

- Automobile Grant: (The **Veterans' Benefits Act of 2010**(**H.R. 3219**, as amended), includes the following:
- Raises an automobile assistance benefit for disabled veterans from $11,000 to $18,900.) Veteran must have a service connected loss of one hand, or one foot, or permanent loss of use of one hand or one foot, or a permanent impairment of vision of both eyes. A veteran must be rated for loss of use before this is granted.
- Payment of special adaptive automobile equipment: In addition to the automobile grant. Veteran must be entitled to the automobile grant as outlined above, or have a service connected ankylosis (immobility) of one knee or one hip. (This requires a VA Doctor's prescription for the adaptive equipment and can include; an automatic transmission, air conditioner, hand controls, power brakes, hand brakes, cruise control, ramps or wheelchair lifts, and any other adaptive equipment the doctor may deem necessary.)

50% SC or Higher, all of the above plus:

- Medical treatment for any condition at VA Medical Centers: Enrollment in a VA health care program is encouraged but not required for treatment of a service connected condition. No co- payments for treatment of non-service connected care or non-service connected prescription drugs.
- Medical treatment in non-VA facilities: for any service connected medical condition with a fee basis card issued to the veteran by an authorized VA Medical Center.

60-90% SC or Higher, all of the above plus:

- Individual Unemployability (increased compensation) payable at the 100% rate based on the inability to work due to service connected disability.

Special Compensation for Severely Disabled

Under a brand new law, certain severely disabled retirees of the uniform services that have a disability rating as reported by the Department of Veterans Affairs (VA) are entitled to special compensation. The special compensation is paid for that month in accordance with the following schedule:

- 70% or 80% = $100.00
- 90% = $200.00
- 100% = $300.00

You must meet the following requirements for entitlement to special compensation for severely disabled:

- You are NOT retired from the military for a disability.
- You are in a retired status and on the retired pay rolls. Members recalled for more than 30 days to active duty are not in a retired status.
- You have 20 or more years of service for the purpose of computing retired pay. A reservist must have 7,200 or more points to qualify.
- The VA rating for disability of 70% or higher must be awarded within 4 years of retirement.

- The VA rating must be 70% or higher for each month. If the rating falls below 70% any given month, then the retiree has no entitlement to special compensation for that month.

When/How You Get Paid

Unlike active duty pay, retired/retainer pay is only paid once per month. Your net retired/retainer pay should be sent to your financial institution by Direct Deposit unless you either reside in a foreign country, which Direct Deposit is not available. Your retired pay will be deposited to your account on the first business day of the month following the end of the month.

Your first payment for retired pay normally will arrive 30 days after your release from active duty, or, on the first business day of the month following the month of first entitlement to pay. In a separate mailing, you will receive a letter which will show you how your pay was computed. This will include your deductions for SBP, federal/state income tax, and allotments.

After you retire, you will need to notify The Defense Finance & Accounting Service (DFAS) whenever you change your financial institution. Do not close your old bank account until you receive the first deposit in the new financial institution.

** This list was compiled from VA Documents, and does not list all benefits a veteran may be eligible for. For further information and/or application procedures concerning these and other benefits consult with the Veterans Affairs at 1-800-827-1000 or proceed to this link: http://www.vba.va.gov/vba/benefits/factsheets/

To Do List for Helpful Transition

o *Primary Care*

✓ Call the **Centralized Scheduling Office** to schedule an intake Primary Care (PCT) appointment(s). You may request to be scheduled at a local CBOC near your primary residence. However, if your clinic of choice is not accepting new patients, please ask to be placed on the electronic waiting list (EWL) for the clinic of your choice and remain open to accepting an appointment at an alternative location. **–If you have already scheduled/attended your initial Primary Care Appt, you can disregard this step.**

✓ **Ask your assigned Primary Care Provider about transfer requests and/or referrals for specialty service line care.** Your provider will need to place a consult for these services. Examples include services lines such as Orthopedics, Pain Management, Occupational Therapy, Physical Therapy, Infectious Disease, Oncology, Audiology, Ophthalmology, Traumatic Brain Injury, Pulmonology, Gastroenterology, Cardiology, and others etc.

✓ Once your information is uploaded to the Atlanta VAMC system, **please confirm you MyHealthEvet (MHV) account is active** and you can access the premium level.

✓ Please present to the **VAMC ER** (here in Atlanta) if you experience a mental health crisis or medical emergency

o *Mental Health*

✓ **Contact the closest VET Center to you,** as walk ins are welcome for Readjustment and other MH Counseling Services. Contact information listed in chart on **pg 4.**

✓ If requested, return to **see Dr. Rogers, the TCM Psychologist** (date scheduled by provider) for your intake mental health appointment. Her phone number is 404-321-6111 ext. **7877.** After completion of the initial assessment, you can be linked with a mental health provider and treatment program that best fits your individual mental health needs.

✓ Call the **Veterans Crisis Line: 1800-273-8255 (TALK)** at any time during the day or night for help with a mental health crisis.

o *Benefits*

✓ **Go to the VBA at 1700 Clairmont Road for applying for VA benefits** including GI Bill benefits (post 911) Vocational Rehabilitation and Employment, and Home Loan Program, pension information, etc. For further information and/or application procedures concerning these and other benefits consult with the Veterans Affairs at 1-800-827-1000 or proceed to this link: http://www.vba.va.gov/vba/benefits/factsheets/

✓ **Follow up with a Veteran Service Organization (VSO)** such as the Disabled American Veterans (DAV) or the State of Georgia Department of Veterans Services for help understanding and accessing benefits, completing applications, enrolling in benefit programs, or seeking advocacy and support regarding military, DOD or benefit related issues.

o *Case Management*

✓ Follow up with **Ms. Kenisha, Case Manager** in the future, if needed regarding other information for point of contacts regarding VA resources and Services. **404-321-6111 ext. 7385.**
Build B: Outpatient Entrance of the Hospital; 2nd floor, across from the main lab

Thank You for Your Service, Welcome Home

"PTSD will not determine how I live in my community and the things I do in life."

A year ago, Curtis Butler III was homeless and sleeping in his car. He attempted suicide twice. This week, he is giving money to those less fortunate.

Butler, forty-five, is a two-tour veteran of the Iraq war who suffers from post-traumatic stress disorder. When he returned home with his disability, he was initially denied benefits, and he fell on hard times. He lost contact with his children. He had no home, no money, and no hope. Twice, he overdosed on pills and alcohol.

"I figured nobody cared about me," Butler told ABC News. "I had to worry about paying bills. I didn't love myself or anyone else."

But Butler finally did get his benefits and turned his life around. On Monday, he made the holidays a little bit easier for two dozen strangers. Butler was standing in line at a Georgia Power office waiting to pay his utility bill. He heard another customer talking about how difficult it had been to make ends meet. He paid that couple's $230 bill and then kept going. When he was finished, he had doled out $2,000 to pay power bills for 20 people.

"This was the anniversary of me being homeless, and now, I am putting smiles on other people's faces," Butler told ABC News.

One woman's power had been turned off at her home because she didn't have any money to pay her bill. Butler paid it for her and then gave her more cash for her children.

"I told her, your kids can't open their presents on Christmas morning with no lights on...

And now, they have more money for food or presents," Butler said.

Genice Harris, a clerk at the Georgia Power office told ABC affiliate WSB that everyone was stunned. "I could tell it was spontaneous, and he was smiling and people were like, 'I can't believe this.' They actually started taking pictures with this guy," Harris said.

She choked back tears as she talked about Butler. "There really is a God and... He does send people to help others that are in need," Harris said.

"I have been there and done it, been close to eating out of trash cans... I was the one on the street with my hand out asking for some change," Butler told ABC News. "God put me in that predicament so that one day I could help others."

Butler has written a book about living with PTSD, and he has a website to promote his efforts advocating new programs for disabled veterans. In his book, "PTSD: My Story, Please Listen!" he writes about returning home and falling on hard times.

"Just because we have PTSD, doesn't mean we are not good people," Butler said. "We come back from fighting in a war and we can't get a job... It is hard to tell your kid that 'I can't support you because I am homeless after fighting for our country.'"

But Butler now is getting the help he needs. He gets counseling through his church. He reconnected with his children. And now he owns an apartment and is about to get married.

"One night, I prayed and I asked God, 'can you reveal to me my wife?' And HE said,

'Yeah stupid, you sit next to [her in] church every Sunday'… God works miracles and wonders every day," Butler said.

This is not the first time he has been a Good Samaritan. Last year, he bought haircuts for 200 homeless vets and the people of his community.

Butler says he knows all about falling on hard times and is happy now that he can be generous with others. As for next year's good deed, Butler hasn't decided. "Me and God are going to talk about that," he said.

(Begin video clip)

HENDRICKS. Some of our service men and women who have already given so much while on active duty keep on giving when they come home. People like Curtis Butler, the once homeless veteran, is paying it forward by helping dozens of Georgia Power customers here in the Atlanta area. Jerry Carnes with CNN affiliate WXIA tells us how. Take a look.

(Begin video clip)

(Laughter)

JERRY CARNES, WXIA CORRESPONDENT. He's at it again.

CURTIS BUTLER III. Doesn't he take credit cards, men?

CARNES. For the second day in a week, Curtis Butler delivers stress relief to those struggling with their bills. Here he encounters a woman whose electricity has been off for a week. Not anymore.

BUTLER. God bless. Merry Christmas.

God can't stop blessing us. So why—why we can't, you know, continue blessing other people.

CARNES. Curtis Butler is not a rich man. He is a military veteran who came home from Iraq with post-traumatic stress. He says he spent some time living in his car on the streets of El Paso, Texas, homeless, until an adjustment in his military benefits brought him to metro Atlanta and his own apartment.

BUTLER. Just being thankful, you know, for what I have. When you can put a smile on somebody's face during the holidays or every day, that's a major blessing.

CARNES. There was shock and tears when Butler entered the Georgia Power building in Stockbridge on Monday and dropped $2,000 to pay the bills of strangers. Michael Guice was one of them.

MICHAEL GUICE, RECEIVED HELP FROM GIVING VETERAN. I was in awe of what happened. And that was—just my first time witnessing how well God works through men.

CARNES. Butler also paid Qiana Cherry's bill, restoring power to her home. There was a little extra for her three-year-old son.

UNIDENTIFIED FEMALE. Thank you!

QIANA CHERRY, RECEIVED HELP FROM GIVING VETERAN: It was like (ph) It's like I hit the lottery or something.

UNIDENTIFIED MALE: You did.

CHERRY: Thank you, Jesus. I thank you God.

CARNES: Curtis Butler came to us wanting to tell his story in hopes of bringing more attention to the plight of veterans facing post-traumatic stress and homelessness.

BUTLER: I did that the way that God wanted me to do.

CARNES: Once homeless himself, Curtis Butler now feels right at home in the arms of generosity.

(End videotape)

HENDRICKS. I love that. That was Jerry Carnes of CNN affiliate WXIA. Joining me now is the man himself, Curtis Butler. It's an honor to meet you.

BUTLER. Good morning, Susan, how are you doing?

HENDRICKS. We saw you giving back and people's initial reaction. How does that feel, to see those people say I feel like I hit the lottery, I now have faith once again. How does that feel?

BUTLER. This is a good feeling because somebody blessed me, and my family has blessed me—when I was on hard luck and once I left El Paso, Texas, the VA hospital, the veterans group that I meet with at the VA Hospital on Wednesdays, they helped me out, the regional office helped me out, David Scott's office. They did a tremendous job. And they were the ones that apologized for what happened to me in El Paso, Texas, and I'm grateful for that.

HENDRICKS. What made you decide, okay, I do want to give back, but I'm paying power bills. I want people to feel like—because, you know, these days with people in a recession, with the US in a recession, people down and out. And as we heard, you're not a rich man. How do you come up with this money to pay it forward?

BUTLER. Well, you know, I have some savings. My fiancée, she helps me save, and she kind of keeps me on track. I just went to pay my light bill. And I kind of ear hustled and heard the older couple said they were having problems paying their bill. So I said, "Excuse me, are you having problem paying your bill?" And they said yes. I said, "I'll pay it for you, Merry Christmas."

HENDRICKS. That is amazing, and I'm sure it makes people then again, want to pay it forward and get back as well. You for a while lived in your car.

BUTLER. Yes.

HENDRICKS. And you were saying that people helped you along the way.

BUTLER. Yes. Once I left El Paso, Texas, I had a friend, a high school buddy of mine, Sergeant First Class Allison Anderson. She told me that one of her soldiers said to have him come here to Atlanta, and they will assist him and help him out, and I'm grateful to both of them also.

HENDRICKS. And you're also helping by writing this book, *Post-Traumatic Stress Disorder, PTSD, My Story. Please listen.* How has that affected you and made you the man you are today? Not only suffering from it but then helping others?

BUTLER. It's like counseling for me, a counseling session for me. And then it's just not for the military. It's also for our civilian counterparts, also the husbands, the wives, the kids. And then, also, you know, big businesses. They don't have to worry—you have to be scared when a soldier has PTSD, and then they say, "Oh, we can't hire you because of the meds that you take." But then I look at it. You know, with PTSD, if we can go down range in a war zone and fight for your freedom and then we come back home and you say, "We can't hire you or, you know, the stuff that you was doing in the military, you have to go to school for that." There should be a way that they can go ahead and transfer, like if you're a medic or if you're a cook or mechanic, transfer those skills into civilian life instead of having a person go back to school again because now it's like they're starting over again. It's redundant.

HENDRICKS. Well said. I'm looking forward to reading your book. What's the main message you wanted to get across? Is that you can survive and live a healthy happy life with PTSD?

BUTLER. Yes. But the main kicker is prayer and then you have to have that person who knows your weak spots. And when they see you in your time of need, they're there to pick you up. And that's what I have in my fiancée and my church and my family and friends.

HENDRICKS. We saw that with you literally paying it forward and paying people's power bill. It really is an honor to meet you. I know quickly you wanted to wish someone a happy birthday?

BUTLER. Yes. Higher Living Bapt—Higher Living Christian Church in Hampton, Georgia. I'd like to give the first lady of the church, Miss...

HENDRICKS. That's okay. It's live TV. Don't worry.

BUTLER. Mrs. Landers, happy birthday, God bless. I love you guys.

HENDRICKS. Curtis Butler, thank you. And I'm looking forward to reading your book as well. You are doing great things.

BUTLER. Yes, ma'am.

HENDRICKS. Good meeting you.

BUTLER. All right.

HENDRICKS. Well, thanks so much for starting your morning with us. We've got much more ahead on CNN Sunday Morning which starts right now.

> Military veteran Curtis Butler, III is no longer homeless, but he isn't wealthy. Still, he's so grateful for having turned his life around that the do-gooder paid some pricey bills for 20 needy customers on Monday.

> "Just being thankful for what I have," Curtis "I'm not rich but when you can put a smile on someone's face, that's a major blessing."

> Butler served in the military from 1989 to 1991 and again from 2002 to 2007, according to his website. When he returned from his final deployment, Butler was diagnosed with PTSD, but because of issues with his benefits, he ended up living in his car in El Paso, Texas for a while, ABC News reports. Butler lost contact with his children and overdosed on pills and alcohol twice.

> But once Butler got his benefits in order, he soon got back on his feet. He returned to school and wrote "PTSD My Story Please Listen!" To raise awareness about the condition and his struggle, according to his website. He now also has an apartment in Henry County, Ga., and is getting ready to get married, 11 Alive reports.

> So when the hopeful veteran came across a couple who couldn't afford their $230 utility bill at Georgia Power on Monday, he was inspired to help and paid the bill for them, according to ABC News. He then bumped into another

woman whose power had been shut off. He gave her money for her bill and some extra cash to buy gifts for her kids.

"I have been there and done it, been close to eating out of trash cans... I was the one on the street with my hand out asking for some change," Butler told ABC News. "God put me in that predicament, so that one day I could help others."

Altogether, Butler handed out more than $2,000 for 20 customers.

"It was an angel sent from heaven," Qiana Cherry, one of the lucky customers, told 11 Alive, "Like I hit the lottery."

STOCKBRIDGE—Imagine standing in line to pay a utility bill and a Good Samaritan pays your bill. That is exactly what happened to several people recently at the Eagle's Landing Stockbridge Georgia Power office.

"I heard this lady and man talking about not being able to pay their bill," said Curtis Butler III. "After I paid their bill, I asked, 'Does anybody in here want their bill paid?' The people said, yes!"

<<Insert image here.>>

Photo by Elaine Rackley

Curtis Butler III is the author of "PTSD: My Story, Please Listen!" The book is an autobiography and features life lessons he learned while in the United States Army.

Butler, 45, said he paid 15 to 20 Georgia Power customers' bills Dec. 3—more than $1,700 overall. He said that day; he stood in between two lines and the customer service window paying bills simultaneously. Butler said he returned the following day and paid three more customers' electric bills.

"It wasn't my call," he said. "It was God's call. I heard God say go ahead and bless them. Now, my book sales are going through the roof since listening to God's voice. When He speaks and you obey, God does things in a major way. When God says bless somebody you do what He says not what man says."

His generosity was born out of a bout with Post Traumatic Stress Disorder, out of being twice homeless and living in his car. In October and November of 2010, his auto was home after being evicted twice.

<<Insert image here.>>

Photo by Elaine Rackley

Curtis Butler III has written a book about dealing with Post Traumatic Stress Disorder following his military career.

Butler has penned a book entitled "PTSD: My Story, Please Listen!" It starts with his childhood and continues through his adult life. Butler said 80 percent of the book is about being in the military and dealing with his daily struggles with PTSD.

Georgia Power spokesperson John Kraft said, Butler's Paying it Forward story is on the company's Facebook and Twitter page.

"It was very generous of him," Kraft said. "It was an action that he took on his own."

Butler said people called him, asking why he did not call them to pay their power bills.

"I told them if I had called you, it wouldn't be the blessing God told me to do," Butler said. "But, thank God I was faithful. I get to help out and bless more veterans. Hopefully we can clean up the streets of homeless veterans."

Butler served in the United States Army Reserve from 1989 until 1991, and a short stint in the U.S. Navy in 1991. He returned to the U.S. Army from 2001 until 2007. He is father to six girls and one boy.

"How do you tell your kids you are homeless after fighting two wars?" Butler asked.

"My bills were totaling $3,000 per month. I was only getting $789 a month," he added.

Butler said he only received that money, which was 50 percent of his veterans disability check. He said he was diagnosed with anxiety in 2007 by Veterans Administration (VA) doctors in El Paso, Texas. Later he was diagnosed with anxiety and (PTSD) by United Behavioral Health doctors in El Paso.

However, the Veterans Administration officials initially denied Butler's Post Traumatic Stress Disorder.

"One doctor said anxiety and the other said I had PTSD, but the VA still denied benefits and kept me at 50 percent of my benefits," he said.

In 2011, the VA apologized about the misdiagnosis, according to Butler.

"I really appreciated that, it took the sting out of the bite a little bit, and that is when I got my benefits," Butler said. "It stormed on me for about four and half years. But now God has rainbows covering me. It is a beautiful thing for my kids. I can bless more homeless veterans now."

Butler said he was able to be a financial blessing to others by using the back payments he received from the VA.

When Henry County renowned rap artist Clifford Harris, better known as "T.I.," heard about Butler's story, he chose the army veteran as the first recipient of his "Give like a King" campaign, according to Nikki Barjon, media representative for "Give like a King."

"This is our first initiative working with homeless veterans with a goal of raising awareness around the issues of veteran homelessness," Barjon said. "It is a global humanitarian campaign to encourage others to give back to the community and get involved."

Barjon said the "Give like a King" campaign team chooses the King of the month. However, it is Harris, who gives the final approval of the team's selection.

"This one was very easy because we followed his paying it forward story in the media," she said. "It was a unanimous decision to recognize him as the first king."

"To live like a king, you must be willing to give like a king. With that being said, it gives me great honor and privilege to give to those who deserve it the most—our veterans," said Harris.

Barjon said they launched the campaign Dec. 14. The campaign will be ongoing and Harris is scheduled to promote the new campaign while on tour.

"T.I. shared that he plans to engage his fans, and work especially hard to inspire younger demographics to get serious about community involvement, humanitarian efforts and giving back," she added.

December 2012 | King of the Month—Curtis Butler

Curtis Butler III, the once homeless military veteran who recently paid dozens of strangers Georgia Power bill in a random act of kindness. Mr. Butler is a soaring example of veterans who fought for our freedom and is continuing to give back as a heroes and beacon of light in our world.

(DERRICK Interview with *PTSD My Story, Please Listen!* author Curtis Butler)

ACKNOWLEDGMENTS

To my wife, Tatina,

We have a long road to continue down, and some days, I know it's rougher than others, and I thank you for being there. I thank you for saying I do when we got married. For one, a lot of information in this book has plenty to do with you on the grounds that you wrote down all of the incidents that occurred, which will be helpful to other veterans and family members, so you are a blessing to me more ways than one, and I appreciate you for that. You were like a detective breaking down my medical notes from the VA. Together with *God*, we can do all things. Every time I look into your pretty brown eyes or listen to you speak, I see and hear the love you have for me, your husband and disabled veteran. Some days, I feel as everyone's against me and that I have to come out fighting. Sometimes, I get upset with you wondering what side or whose side you are on. At times, I'm so dog on confused that I don't know if I'm coming or going. I feel like I'm in a straitjacket and can't move or breathe because of the situation I've been put in. I apologize for being difficult at times, and I am working on me, and it's a struggle. People give advice and never walked a mile in my shoes, so to me, I feel like I'm being slapped in the face. I think people say things to you just to see if they can push my button. You know I fight with trust issues and don't want to feel as if I'm a charity case; it's hard for me to put the right words together, if that makes any sense. I do thank you for all you do and appreciate what you've done and continue to do.

Love,
Curtis Butler III

*****

In this book, my wife and I wrote approximate times of the events that happen to the best of our knowledge, and this book is to assist in the process of your paperwork for your disabilities. This book is for informational purpose only; there are no implicit or explicit guarantees that you will be successful in your case by using the information contained in this book. We have to continue to get our congressional people and senators along with the veterans administration hospital and regional office to work for us and not against us and vice versa. We have to change their mindsets by reading Title 38 Federal Rules and Regulation and C.O.V.A. courts of veterans appeals on the grounds that your situation may be the same that they ruled for in another veteran's case. Go to the veterans representative, just because I had a not so good run with them; they may work for you differently. Ask questions, take notes, continue to educate yourself so that you can take better care of your family. Stay away from the *appeal* due to the longevity of the process only if you can and if it does not put you into a hardship. Do a letter of reconsideration, this is much quicker counting on a case-by-case situation.

Just remember when was the last time you saw a homeless general? It's always been the lower enlisted probably the ones who trained the officers, and some who did not train them. The point is we all served in war time and peace time, what happen to we will leave no soldier behind. I would say we all failed them approximately 600,000 homeless battle buddies, but we are the best country, the great USA. Now, I ask how can we put those two in the same sentence and feel good. Am I the only one that see the disgrace in what we did; I say this as it's up to us and then we inform our government. We cannot blame the government only we have a voice, our government does whatever we let them get away with. This has to stop. These suicides of veterans with family members, President Obama or whoever the next president is, what do you think about this? Do you sleep well at night? I would love to sit down and speak with you in order to resolve this tsunami that is spreading fast like cancer. We need a bill for our veterans; we need a right now for many of our men and women who are dying after returning from the battlefield due to the lack of treatment, complexity, and deceit. Mr. President, why haven't anyone been prosecuted for these suicides of our *heroes*? But they continue to receive paychecks knowing that those veterans had PTSD? America is awaiting an answer, let's meet and talk. Your place or mine. I've been hearing this peanut butter and jelly sermon for a while. Let's sit down and bounce ideas off of one another so that we can take care of the VA, regional offices, and homeless veterans disaster that is looking more and more like a tsunami.

Thank you, God, for the people you brought into our lives.

First, I would like to thank *God* who is the head of my household. Thank you for guiding me and putting God-fearing people into our lives so that we can do your work in order for you to get all the glory. My pastor and copastor teach us we cannot be a church unless we are in the community serving Gods' people. What an awesome man and woman of *God*. Thank you to my editors, retired (LTC) Kevin Gainer and retired (Major) Joseph Martin, for your phone calls, meetings, and your knowledgeable input. To comedian Willie Brown and wife, Sherry Brown, thank you both for the talks and prayers to my wife and I. Ministers Mitch and Gloria Mormon, thank you for allowing us to come to your home so that you both could minister to us. To retired (CSM) Aaron Martin and retired (LTC) Lisha Florence, thank you both for being there for my family when times were dark and gloomy. To Michael Guice and family, thank you for supplying me with much needed information to help restore my faith. Thank you to Erica Walker for showing me so much love during our interviews; Ryan Cameron, Wanda Smith, Big Tigger and the whole V-103 *The People's Station* and *News & Talk* 1380 WAOK,

Dr. Rashad Richey and staff. Thank you to Susanne Hendricks from CNN here in Atlanta, Georgia, for the interview; *ABC News* with Diane Sawyer, staff member Beth Loyd; and Dr. Lehome Bliss for assisting with the phone interview. Thank you, 11Alive News interviews with Jerry Carnes and Keith Whitney here in Atlanta, Georgia, for our many interviews. Thank you, T.I. and Tiny, for naming me "King of the Month" for paying it forward; it is an honor. Thank you to Raymond and Sandra James for dropping everything and coming to a soldier's side at the hospital and praying for me when I was feeling my lowest when my blood pressure was over 180 with migraines. Thank you to London and Janet Hill for going with my wife and myself to the hospital when my migraine pushed my blood pressure over 170. To retired (Major) Joseph Martin and family, thank you for the love and support to my family. Author Tracy Dyson, thank you for your input on the book and many phone calls with my brother, your words along with lunch has blessed me in so many ways. Again, thank you. Thank you to my mentors. The Anthony's from "THISISITBBQ" "IT'S THE RIB TIPS;" it's an Atlanta Georgia, thing. You guys are such a blessing to my family and the community. Thank you, Sheriff Victor Hill, Senator Gayle Davenport, Chief Gregory Porter, Commissioner Shana M. Rooks, Chairman Jeffrey Turner, my good friends of Clayton County, Georgia. Thank you, Congressman David Scott and staff; you guys did not leave me hanging. You fought the battle with me from beginning to end, and my family appreciates your tireless efforts. Thank you also goes out to Senator Johnny Isakson's staff. To the University of Phoenix in Decatur, Georgia, Sandy Springs Georgia, El Paso, Texas, and Santa Teresa, New Mexico instructors and staff; it's been seven years, but we've done it with disabilities, homelessness, and moving to another state while I continue to fight for my disability benefits. *God* is good. I will receive my BSB/A October 2015. Thank you and *God* bless you all. Andrew and Dimitri from the University of Phoenix in Arizona, special thanks for keeping my schedule tight and my classes paid on time. Thank you to Hartmut Mueller and Patricia Sias of El Paso, Texas, for assisting with my book and having a great heart for your veterans. Thank you to my Brooklyn Brother Minister Craig Merritt of *Mind II Concepts* for the book cover photos and for giving my daughter, Nia, good business information on being photogenic at photo shoots. To my brother actor, Justin Merritt, thank you for speaking to my daughter, Nia, on how to present herself to talent agents. To Rose Merritt, thank you for always welcoming us into your home; you are such a blessing. Thank you to the people at the director's office at the regional building, along with the disabled American veteran and the VA Hospital in Decatur, Georgia. Again, there are some people working for the veterans, and I will continue to pray that we get a hundred percent of the staff all over the world to make the veterans feel welcomed and appreciated and respected after doing such a noble job and giving so much to their country. Thank you to the veteran service officers (VSO) in Griffin, Georgia; DAV Chapter 1 in Henry County, Georgia; DAV Chapter 92 in Decatur, Georgia. Thank you to the NAACP in Henry County. Thank you also goes out to my friend, my brother, my mentor, Minister Charlie Pugh and his staff at the Georgia Department of Labor for all the hard work and dedication they give to our veterans seven days a week (this is not a type o). To my people at Dre and Craig's VIP CUTZ, thank you Blu for keeping me groomed. Thanks goes out to Jae Ellis, Big Will, thanks for keeping me fresh for 11 Alive News, V103 FM Radio, ABC News, and CNN News interviews. Reggie's Barbershop, to include Stan and Comedian Dr. Foolish Nelson. Paul Winfrey, my other mentor and neighbor, thank you for keeping my family and me in the know on events for the veterans to always help improve themselves with knowledge. Michael T. Daytes, for the YouTube interview and photos of my first free haircut to the homeless veterans and soldiers in my community, thank you, my brother. Job well done. To Bobby and Deidre Hill, London and Janet Hill, Sid and Althea Johnson, Guy and Barbara Allen, Bill and Brigette Brown, Tony and Michelle, thank you for supporting us as we celebrate our fifth-year wedding anniversary. Thank you to my attorneys at the Deming Law Firm in Duluth, Georgia. My dentist Dr. Bilbro and staff in El Paso, Texas, and Dr. Brooks and staff in McDonough, Georgia. A special thank-you goes out to my advisor at the University of Phoenix where I began as a student in El Paso, Texas. Glen Garcia, when I wanted to give up, you kept pushing me, and now I'm graduating October 2015. Thank you, Glen for showing a veteran love and thanks for the letter you sent to the media outlet and to the university staff and higher-ups at the University of Phoenix. You are a forever friend and part of the Butler family, thank you and many blessings to you and your family. To retired (LTC) Kevin Gainer and family, thank you also for assisting Tatina and myself with this book, the many phone calls and e-mails, the editing and mentoring. Thank you to Lovejoy Police Department Chief W. Woods for helping my family and me in time of need. Thank you to Susan Bowie, director at WAGA FOX 5 Atlanta Call for Action for your calls, e-mails, and concerns for a veteran. Thank you to the Kappa Lambda Chi Military Fraternity, Inc.– Atlanta Epsilon Chapter, WAYPOINT in Griffin, Georgia, National Association for Black Veterans, Inc. in Griffin, Georgia, Hunger Has No Religion. Thank you to Dr. Lehome Bliss and Albert Bliss of The Bliss Center... Relax. To my cousin Judge Greg Mathis, can you give me some advice or contacts to help change the laws on veterans who have served whether with an honorable or bad conduct discharge? They did serve so that their families could receive benefits. We would appreciate this; some would say I'm crazy, but in my heart, this is the right thing to do.

Everyone I thanked we are so appreciative of you all and thank you for blessing my family, and we hope to be a blessing to everybody *God* Bless.

I would like to thank my family for their support; my beautiful wife, Tatina; my kids, Danielle, Setaga, Sharniece, Latasha, Nia, Shamar, Adrionna, Brionna, and Miranda; and my twelve grandkids. I love them like crazy. My in-laws, what can I say, I hit the power ball. They're awesome. The wisdom this family has from mom and dad, my brothers and sisters-in-law and my nieces and nephews, I am blessed to know and have the McKays and the Mcleods in my life. To Pastor Norman and family, thank you for the word and blessings, rest in paradise, sir, until we meet again. Grandma, Granddad,

Aunt Mary Butler, Aunt Amina Bayyon, Uncle Tony Spencer, thank you for your guidance and many prayers that you bestowed on my life. I love you and miss you sadly. Rest in paradise. Thank you, mom and dad since we are past the storms in life, now, we can love one another like crazy. To my aunts, uncles, cousins, brothers, sisters, nieces, and nephews, you are so awesome, and I appreciate the support and am honored to be a part of this wonderful family. To Kool & the Gang, thank you for all you do by changing the world with your music; I pray I can change some things also for our veterans and soldiers who protect our *freedom* on a daily. Hakim Bell holla at me cousin. Rest in paradise to the meanest guitarist, Charles Smith, and trombonist, Clifford Adams, of Kool & the Gang. RIP to the Charleston 9; I lost family and friends at the AME Church in Charleston, South Carolina—Clementa Pinckney, Tywanza Sanders, Daniel Simmons, Sharonda Singleton, Myra Thompson, Cynthia Hurd, Suzie Jackson, Ethel Lance, and DePayne Middleton-Doctor. Rest in peace, Mitch Mormon Jr., Sid Johnson, Minister Harvey Sturdivant, cousin Sakinah Debra Bell, and Grandma Corena R. Norman McKay, age 103.

RESOURCES FOR ATTORNEYS

http://www.priceboydlaw.com/attorney/andrea-boyd-esq/

Attorneys: Volunteer—Veterans Consortium Pro Bono Program

www.vetsprobono.org/volunteer-today/

Lawyers volunteer to provide pro bono representation for veterans and their dependents or survivors in their appeal before the U.S. Court of Appeals for.

A Summary of the Pro Bono Program—What Does a Volunteer Commit To?

Hiring a VA-Certified Veterans Disability Lawyer—Nolo.com

www.nolo.com/legal.../hiring-va-certified-disability-lawyer.ht..

Nolo.com

You should consult with a veterans disability lawyer if you're appealing a denial... TheVeterans Consortium Pro Bono Program provides free representation to.

HOW TO Hire A Veterans Law Attorney—VA Watchdog

https://www.vawatchdog.org/how-to-hire-a-veterans-law-attorney.html

Ten Years of Service to America's Military Veterans. Since 2005 This Is The Site VA Reads When They. Want To Learn What They've Been Doing. Welcome...

Lawyers Announce Free Help for Veterans

militaryadvantage.military.com/.../veterans-get-free-help-fr...

Military.com

May 27, 2011—With the recent push, the ABA is asking attorneys to donate time and services... For those veterans seeking help, please click on the "Pro Bono...

McElreath & Stevens, LLC

Atlanta Veterans Disability Attorney
513 Edgewood Ave SE Suite 100
Atlanta, GA 30312
Phone: (888) 640-0051
Local: (404) 467-9017
http://www.atlantaveteransdisabilityattorney.com/
National Organization of Veterans' Advocates (NOVA)
https://vetadvocates.org
The National Organization of Veterans' Advocates, Inc. (NOVA) is
    a... NOVA NamesVeterans Attorney Diane Boyd Rauber as
    Director of Legislative and...
http://www.veteranslaw.com/consultation-request
https://www.va.gov/homeless/docs/HCHV_Sites_ByState.pdf
Resources for Veteran out Reach
American Legion 516, McDonough Georgia
Congressional Office
Disabled American Veterans
Georgia Department of Labor (Charlie Pugh)
Hunger Has No Religion (Founder Donny Edwards) dedwards@
    hungerhasnoreligion.org
National Association for Black Veterans, Inc. (NABVETS)
    Commander Willie J. Brantley BS Pysch, VSR, CPS, CARES
    770-504-6945
Purple Heart
Senators Office
Vet Center
Vets.com
Veterans of Foreign Wars
Veterans Service Officers
WAYPOINT in Griffin, Ga (MSG) Sandra Brownlee (Ret) dsp-
    2mandm@gmail.com
Wounded Warrior Project

McELREATH & STEVENS, LLC
ATTORNEYS AT LAW

www.atlantadisability.com
www.atlantaveteransdisabilityattorney.com

Attorneys
David A. Stevens
Douglas E. Sullivan
Licensed in MA

Of Counsel
Jane S. McElreath

513 Edgewood Avenue
Suite 100
Atlanta, GA 30312

404-467-9017 phone
404-467-8992 fax

Engagement Letter

Thank you for entrusting us with your VA disability benefits claim. We appreciate your service and dedication to our country.

It is important to note some of the common problems that veteran's face during this process and what you can do to help.

1- Be patient. Cases, on average, take years before they are resolved. We ask for your understanding of the fact that we do not have the ability to speed up this process unless you have been diagnosed with a **terminal illness or have a letter threatening eviction.**

2- Be sure to contact your Congressman. You are encouraged to contact your Congressman and request a **letter of inquiry** into the status of your case.

3- Be skeptical regarding other sources of information. E-Benefits and the 1-800-827-1000 VA Benefits Help Line often give inaccurate information. **Please check with our office** before trusting those sources of information or call us for any clarification.

4- Be sure to verify VA statements. If a VA employee tells you that they cannot assist you with a question relating to your claim because you have an attorney, they are mistaken. Ask for his or her name and phone number and we will inform them of the law.

5- Be aware that representatives from organizations working at the VA Regional Office, such as the DAV or VFW, are not representatives of the VA. **Please contact us** if you have any questions.

6- Be mindful that the VA makes mistakes. Occasionally, the VA will fail to process a piece of information. However, **we can correct these mistakes.** We make sure to receive a receipt for every submission to the VA, however, the VA regularly takes months to process these submissions.

7- Be vigilant. If you receive **any correspondence from the VA, please call** us. The VA has failed to send our office correspondence in the past. Together, we can make sure that nothing falls between the cracks.

Our goal is to resolve your case and provide you with the compensation that you deserve. Your full understanding and cooperation will allow us to dedicate the fullness of our time to the legal questions posed by your case and our other veterans' cases.

Cartersville Office: 112 Stonewall Street, Cartersville, GA 30120. 770-386-6767, Fax 770-386-2939

This engagement letter begins our attorney-client relationship. The information that you share with this office is confidential. If you wish for us to share any information with a spouse or other family member, please indicate that to us so that we may update your file accordingly.

Due to the length of time involved with your case, there are periods where we must wait for the VA to act. During this period there is no new information to share with you, and while we may not contact you during one of these periods, we continue to work on your case. We encourage you to call us if you have any questions or concerns with your case and each time the VA sends you correspondence.

Finally, the fee agreement that we signed authorizes us to receive a fee upon your receipt of retroactive benefits even if you terminate our representation at a later date. Our representation and our ability to receive a fee extends to all disability benefits claims, including those filed prior to our engagement.

The signatures required below are an acknowledgement of the information contained in this engagement letter and an agreement to pursue these objectives in good faith.

X _____   _____
Client's Printed Name   Attorney's Printed Name

X _____   _____
Client's Signature   Attorney's Signature

_____   _____
Date   Date

EMERGENCY TELEPHONE
NUMBERS

These are more effective than 911. Call when:

1. You are sad. (John 14)
2. You have sinned. (Psalm 51)
3. You are facing danger. (Psalm 91)
4. People have failed you. (Psalm 27)
5. It feels as though God is far from you. (Psalm 139)
6. Your faith needs stimulation. (Hebrews 11)
7. You are alone and scared. (Psalm 23)
8. You are worried. (Matthew 8:19–34)
9. You are hurt and critical. (1Corinthians 13)
10. You wonder about Christianity. (2 Corinthians 5:15–18)
11. You feel like an outcast. (Romans 8:31–39)
12. You are seeking peace. (Matthew 11:25–30)
13. It feels as if the world is bigger than God. Psalm 90
14. You need Christ like insurance. (Romans 8:1–30)
15. You are praying for yourself. (Psalm 87)
16. You lose faith in mankind. (Corinthians 13)
17. It looks like people are unfriendly. (John 15)
18. You are losing hope. (Psalm 126)
19. Dealing with fear (Psalm 3:47)
20. For security (Psalm 121:3)
21. For assurance (Mark 8:35)
22. For reassurance (Psalm 145:18)

Gofundme awards and thank you for the people making this possible. About $10 will receive a digital copy of the book when it's released.

Tony Levine—$25
Joan Williams—$20
Judge Chaundra Lewis—$20
Mr. Dee—$25
Margie Saenz—$10
Carla Broussard $25
Bonita Feaster Johnson—$25
Portia Mariee—$20
Dana Butler—$30
Gwendolyn Hockley—$20
Deborah—$10
Marvin Brown—$35
Danielle Scott—$10
Carla Williams—$20
J Coach Brown—$25
Deacon and Minister Hardy—$20
Joseph Dolby—$25
Chefdabo and Gabrielle Jenkins—$25
Antonio—$20
Jessie Jenkins—$25
$100 will receive a signed copy of the book, and you will be listed as a Silver Sponsor.
Charlene Scott—$125
Fred Walker—$100

Jeanette Spencer—$100

$500 will receive a signed copy of the book, and you will be listed as a Gold Sponsor.

$1000 will receive a signed copy of the book, and you will be listed as a Platinum Sponsor.

Curtis Butler III—$2785

Our government wages for life.
Soldiers wage not all for life.
I never voted for this. Is our government bigger than God?
This lets me know our government is about self.

WAGES

Salary of retired US
Presidents............................$450,000 FOR LIFE
Salary of House/Senate
members.......................$174,000 FOR LIFE
Salary of Speaker of the
House............................$223,500 FOR LIFE
Salary of Majority/Minority
Leaders......................$194,400 FOR LIFE

Average salary of a soldier DEPLOYED IN
AFGHANISTAN $38,000

Average income for Seniors on Social Security
......................$12,000

I think we found where the cuts should be made!

If you agree...Pass it on!

ABOUT THE AUTHOR

When my tour was over, I went back home to visit family and friends as well as to meet my dad at the 369th Infantry Regiment, Harlem Hellfighters National Guard Armory in Harlem, New York. They were loading up and getting ready to head out to Fort Dix, New Jersey, for their tour of duty in Baghdad, Iraq. Once we got there and his unit was locked down until they head out, I briefed my dad, along with some of his soldiers, on the dangers. For instance, I told them, "If you didn't put it down, don't pick it up. The insurgents love to place booby traps. You will also be on the road to BIAP, which is IED alley. Make sure you place sandbags on the floor of all of your vehicles, scan your area, and be at the ready. When getting out of your vehicles, watch your step. If there is a full moon, it will brighten up the sky, which lets the insurgents see movement on the base clearly. You will have incoming of rockets, mortar rounds, and small arms fire. At approximately 20:00 hours or 8:00 p.m. on some days, you will get attacked with rockets, mortar rounds, and small arms fire. On holidays, mornings and afternoon, you will get attacked. Keep your vehicles well maintained and your weapons cleaned and eat right and drink plenty of water and pray." I told them to be safe and said to my dad, "Love you, man." And he replied, "Love you too."

My dad's unit got to Kuwait and got causalities, and when they arrived in Baghdad, Iraq, they had causalities on the IED alley which I briefed them on. I walked past some of those soldiers at the armory, and I still have the news article of those incidents, and I sit back with tears in my eyes and thank them for their service to our country.

Rest in peace to all of the soldiers and Marines who gave all for freedom and peace! Your tour has ended. *Rest!*

P—*Proud*
T—*Tough*
S—*Strong*
D—*Determined*

CPSIA information can be obtained
at www.ICGtesting.com
Printed in the USA
LVHW020005270520
656402LV00006B/352